D1564873

A HISTORY OF
PROFESSIONAL HOCKEY
IN MINNESOTA

FROM THE NORTH STARS TO THE WILD

GEORGE REKELA

THE
History
PRESS

Published by The History Press
Charleston, SC 29403
www.historypress.net

First published 2014

ISBN 978-1-5402-0966-5

Library of Congress CIP data applied for.

CONTENTS

INTRODUCTION

H ockey is Canada's national game.

Ask any Canadian, and he or she probably will tell you that Canadians invented the sport. While this may or may not be accurate, we do know that a group of Canadians did invent the National Hockey League (NHL) and dominated it from the NHL's inception in 1917 to the latter part of the twentieth century.

In its first year of operation, the NHL boasted organized teams in the key Canadian cities of Toronto, Montreal and Ottawa. Other teams came and went, including the departure of Ottawa, until 1942, the first year of the so-called Original Six: Montreal, Toronto, Detroit, New York, Boston and Chicago. During the years from 1942 to 1967, despite the presence of four American teams in the league, the two Canadian teams dominated. Montreal and Toronto each won ten Stanley Cup championships, and Detroit, next door to Windsor, Ontario, won five. Nearly all NHL players hailed from Canada. Little thought was given to rocking the boat.

Then something happened that would change everything.

In 1958, Branch Rickey, former president and general manager of the Brooklyn Dodgers and the man who brought Jackie Robinson into organized baseball, proposed creation of a new professional baseball association to compete with the American and National Leagues. This led to the somewhat unintended consequence of triggering expansion in both those leagues, an event that had previously not happened in the twentieth century.

Baseball in 1958 was truly America's national pastime, as witnessed by a Gallup Poll revealing that 32 percent of U.S. citizens chose baseball as their favorite sport, while 21 percent selected football and 10 percent basketball. Hockey was one of the less-than-10 percent crowd that included soccer and horseshoes.

Baseball's commissioner, Ford Frick, "presided over a domain that for decades had managed to endure as the nation's game, despite the absence of a prevailing organizational logic, a vision of the future, a governing voice, or a conscience," wrote Michael Shapiro in his book *Bottom of the Ninth*. That lack of conscience had allowed Walter O'Malley and Horace Stoneham to move their New York City teams to Los Angeles and San Francisco, respectively.

Rickey's proposed new league, the Continental, consisting of teams representing New York, Toronto, Houston, Atlanta, Dallas, Denver and Minneapolis, never got off the ground. But it can be persuasively argued that it triggered expansion in football, basketball and hockey.

Baseball's overlords, ever fearful of congressional action, were spooked, in part, into expansion by U.S. senator Estes Kefauver (D-Tennessee) and his Antitrust and Monopolies investigation subcommittee. The American League jumped first, expanding to Los Angeles and Minneapolis–St. Paul in 1961.

In the first of several byzantine expansion maneuvers to come, Minnesota did not get an expansion team. The Twin Cities got a fully formed one, the Washington Senators. American League president Joe Cronin gave his blessing to transferring Calvin Griffith's up-and-coming young Washington team to the Upper Midwest. Interestingly, Cronin and Griffith were related by marriage.

Of the remaining Continental League cities, Toronto and Denver had to wait, but Buffalo won't get a major-league team until the day certain warm subterranean nether regions freeze. The District got an expansion franchise to assuage congressional watchdogs, present and future. The "new" Washington Senators eventually found their way to Dallas–Fort Worth and became the Rangers when Congress wasn't looking. By then, New York, Houston and Atlanta had National League teams. Of the remaining Continental League cities, Denver had to wait until 1993.

If baseball's overlords were obtuse, the NHL was guilty of operating in a vacuum. But as for the National Football League, expansion was more or less forced when, in 1950, to avoid competition, the NFL absorbed All-American Conference teams operating out of San Francisco, Cleveland,

Baltimore and New York. The first two, the 49ers and the Browns, were rousing successes—the other two, not so much. The original Baltimore Colts folded. The New York franchise was shifted to Dallas, where it failed spectacularly. Attendance at the Cotton Bowl was sparse, and the Dallas Texans finished the season playing all road games. The following year, the Texans were moved to Baltimore. Given a second chance, the fans of Baltimore eventually rallied about the team, and attendance soared. Nevertheless, NFL officials were as leery as their NHL counterparts about expansion and busied themselves with shoring up the existing twelve franchises, thanks in part to a new television deal with CBS.

Only when threatened with another new league—the American Football League in 1960—did the NFL expand again. League officials then sought to knock the pins out of the AFL by awarding franchises to two keystone metro areas: Dallas–Fort Worth and Minneapolis–St. Paul.

And so in 1961, the Twin Cities were major-league again. And not a minute too soon, for the region had been devastated by the loss of its beloved team, the Minneapolis Lakers, gone to Los Angeles in 1960. Thus, for a brief period, none of the four major professional leagues had a Twin Cities team. The void, however, was filled that autumn by the intense popularity of the national champion University of Minnesota football Golden Gophers.

In the spring of 1961, the Minnesota Twins arrived from Washington, D.C. Later, the Minnesota Vikings set up training camp in Bemidji, Minnesota, prior to opening the NFL season against the Chicago Bears at Metropolitan Stadium in Bloomington.

The Lakers' departure signaled a period of relative stability in the National Basketball Association. Establishing a team in the nation's second-largest media market was crucial in the league shifting teams from middle-tier cities such as Fort Wayne and Rochester while holding tight to a core of eight teams. The NBA in 1961 did try to establish a beachhead in Chicago with the Packers, but that venture was doomed to failure. The Packers drew few fans and then became the Zephyrs and drew even fewer, eventually moving to Baltimore. The NBA had tried expansion and got burned.

The National Hockey League, however, was to go on to try something completely different, and the Twin Cities were invited to go along for the ride.

The NHL was not oblivious to expansion, merely cautious. Team owners Stafford Smythe (Montreal) and Howard Ballard (Toronto) were vocal in their opposition. A feeble attempt to make Cleveland the seventh NHL team in 1951 was rejected by the NHL board of governors, and any further expansion talk was squelched for the balance of the decade.

According to the *New York Times*, the league was playing to 95.7 percent of capacity. The four American cities had a few Saturday games televised on CBS, and Toronto and Montreal had a lucrative contract with the Canadian Broadcasting Network (CBC). The feeling was that if it ain't broke, don't fix it.

Six teams made up the NHL from 1942 to 1967, but only three dominated. Two were in Canada, and the third had a Canadian metropolis next door. The NHL had a rule that each league member had exclusive rights to any player residing within a fifty-mile radius. In the pre-expansion era, the vast majority of the NHL on the ice and in the front office were Canadian, and Smythe and Ballard, owners of the most successful franchises, didn't want to rock their boat.

On their side was Clarence Campbell, NHL president and a fellow Canadian. "Increasing the league doesn't increase revenue five cents per club," Campbell said. "Right now we're a pretty successful operation."

Campbell indicated any expansion would simply create "more hockey," and all of it "diluted."

"Almost since its inception," wrote Ken Campbell in the *Hockey News*, "the NHL has been dominated by owners whose self-interests always trumped those of the collective. NHL president Clarence Campbell often pointed out making the league bigger would not sell a single ticket in the Original Six markets because all those tickets had been sold anyway."

So what happened to change the minds of these powerful Canadians? America's Pacific Coast, specifically Southern California, had been seen as a version of El Dorado to professional sports leagues. Millions of Americans had moved to California since World War II. Demands for goods, services and jobs were being met. Some of the transplanted easterners had even experienced professional hockey.

The profit motive had caused the Cleveland Rams to become the Los Angeles Rams, the Brooklyn Dodgers to become the Los Angeles Dodgers and the Minneapolis Lakers to become the improbably named Los Angeles Lakers. As noted sportscaster Howard Cosell was fond of saying: "Los Angeles is the city of stolen sports franchises."

The NHL was locked into six cities. California might have been appealing, but none of the Original Six was willing to relocate. If Los Angeles were to get an NHL franchise, the league would have to expand, and expansion, at first, was not in the works.

However, the Western Hockey League (WHL), pro hockey's top minor league, did have a team in Los Angeles, the Blades, a moneymaking venture operated out of the Los Angeles Sports Arena, then home of the Lakers. Taking a page from Branch Rickey, Los Angeles Blades' co-owner Dan Reeves proposed elevation of the WHL to major-league status in direct competition with the NHL. The WHL teams included the San Francisco Seals, the Seattle Totems, the Vancouver Canucks, the Portland Buckaroos and the Victoria Maple Leafs. A team representing Victoria won the Stanley Cup in 1925. Vancouver teams were Stanley Cup runners-up in 1918, 1921, 1922, 1923 and 1924. Seattle was a finalist in 1920 and was tied with Montreal in 1919 when the series was cancelled due to the infamous influenza epidemic in the United States and Canada.

Reeves, co-owner of the Los Angeles Blades with James Piggot, also owned the popular Los Angeles Rams NFL franchise. The threat of a new major league headquartered in Los Angeles resulted in the NHL bosses giving the city more than a casual glance, but travel expenses (the closest league city was Chicago) prevented further discussion. Also, a seven-team league would create scheduling problems.

But what if there was a second California city was added to the mix? Two expansion teams instead of one would economize on travel and even create a rivalry between the two. Air travel was becoming more convenient. Coast-to-coast travel was even less expensive than in the recent past. Airplanes now had pressurized cabin space. Long-distance flying was now a breeze with competition between United, American and TWA improving service.

San Francisco was seen as a viable second expansion city. After all, the New York baseball Giants had moved to the Golden State along with the Dodgers, easing travel expenses for National League baseball teams. And the NBA cut expenses by moving the Warriors from Philadelphia to San Francisco in 1962.

Still, the NHL was frozen in indecision. But even Clarence Campbell saw the light. "Expansion is inevitable," he said. "With a show as good as ours, economics someday may induce or force expansion."

The National Hockey League "finally decided to expand in an effort to achieve two goals—to thwart any possibility of a rival league and to pursue a national television contract," wrote Ken Campbell. "It failed miserably on both accounts."

By any measure of logic, expansion to two California cities and enlarging the NHL from six teams to eight seemed prudent. The league would be split into two divisions, East and West. Any further expansion would proceed at a moderate pace. The results of expansion could be measured and carefully weighed before going forward in the same conservative way the league had operated since 1942.

What the league did instead shocked the world of professional sports.

Chapter 1
NO PLACE TO PLAY

If the NHL was to expand by adding two West Coast cities, many Canadians saw Vancouver, rather than San Francisco, as the likely site. In a league controlled by Canadian interests, another Canadian city seemed likely. However, despite the support of mayor William Rathie, a proposed $8 million, twenty-thousand-seat arena in downtown Vancouver had been rejected by voters.

The March 11, 1965 announcement by Clarence Campbell that the league would expand by not by two but by six cities was greeted by shock and anticipation. Surely one of those six cities would be Canadian. The likely choice would be Vancouver.

Not so fast, said Campbell. Applications would be accepted from responsible groups representing "major-league cities" in the United States and Canada.

At the time, major-league cities were defined as those possessing big-league professional baseball and NFL football teams. Vancouver had neither. Nevertheless, Cyrus McLean, chairman of BC Telephone and head of a group known as Burrard Hockey Club Ltd., submitted a bid in the name of Vancouver.

However, the Minneapolis–St. Paul region was major-league with the Twins and the Vikings, both ensconced at Metropolitan Stadium since 1961. Into the scene stepped Walter Bush, president of the Central Professional Hockey League's (CPHL) Minneapolis Bruins. A Minneapolis real estate attorney, Bush had also served as manager of the 1964 U.S. Olympic hockey team.

Bush helped organize the CPHL and was largely responsible for what turned out to be one of the few successful minor leagues of that era. St. Paul also had a CPHL team, the Rangers. Bush indicated that Minneapolis would likely make an application for an NHL franchise, but the Bruins' home ice (the smelly, old Minneapolis Arena) was not suitable for major-league hockey. "We don't have a place to play," he lamented. Other Twin Cities venues mentioned were in St. Paul: the downtown Auditorium and the State Fair Coliseum.

Meanwhile, the hockey world was aghast at the notion that the NHL, after decades of ossification, was going to double its size. "It is entirely understandable," wrote Ken Campbell in the *Hockey News*, "to view those who run hockey as myopic and greedy."

Now those myopic and greedy men had undergone a transformation. They were going expansion crazy all at once. "Nothing of its kind was seen before or since," wrote Campbell.

Thirteen entities submitted franchise bids, along with $10,000 deposits, to the NHL. The figure is somewhat misleading because five of the applications came from individual groups in Los Angeles and two from Pittsburgh interests. Two Minnesota groups (one from Minneapolis and the other from St. Paul) arrived separately, each planning to make singular presentations at the board of governors meeting, but were told to forget it. "The two delegations," wrote Bill Boni in the *St. Paul Pioneer Press*, "learned that they would be cutting each other's throats if they came in with separate pitches."

As much as it might have galled certain individual delegation members, Minneapolis and St. Paul had to cast aside previous rivalries to put forth a united front. This simplified matters in that, as Bush had indicated, the Minneapolis delegation had no existing arena to show off to the board of governors. The St. Paul delegation had the downtown St. Paul Auditorium, site of the increasingly popular State High School Hockey Tournament.

So at 2:30 p.m. on February 8, 1966, the newly formed Minneapolis–St. Paul delegation, headed by Bush, proudly marched into the meeting, made its presentation and was turned down flat.

"We kept pitching [an expanded] St. Paul Auditorium, but they didn't want to listen," Bush said later.

Especially vocal were brothers James D. and Bruce Norris, who owned the Chicago Blackhawks and Detroit Red Wings, respectively. According to Bush, the Norris boys "kept saying they weren't interested...so we said we would build, and this is what they wanted to hear."

According to Boni, the Twin Cities delegation "ran into marked NHL sentiment against [the St. Paul Auditorium] and in favor of constructing a new facility."

Backed into a corner, the delegation came up with a building site that was "not even completely on paper," Boni wrote. Bush told the NHL that his group would build a suitable NHL arena in the parking lot of Metropolitan Stadium in Bloomington, Minnesota, home of the Twins and Vikings.

"We actually presented one of the weaker cases of any of the towns," Bush said. He listed Los Angeles, San Francisco, Pittsburgh and Baltimore as the favorites to win the expansion lottery. The Metropolitan Stadium site had no architect, no engineer and no contactor. The site fell under the control of the Metropolitan Sports Authority Commission, whose chairman, Gerald Moore, said, "My first concern is building a new left field grandstand."

Yet when the six cities were announced, Minneapolis–St. Paul was there along with Los Angeles, San Francisco, Pittsburgh, Philadelphia and St. Louis. Baltimore didn't make the cut. (The city was destined to lose out on all future NHL expansion.)

The Minneapolis–St. Paul franchise was "conditional." The condition was the Bush group had to have a new arena ready for the 1967–68 NHL season.

For the Philadelphia group, the announcement came as a pleasant surprise. "There was nothing in the Philadelphia papers about the NHL plan for expansion," said Ed Snider, who headed the group representing the City of Brotherly Love. "As far as the papers here, the NHL doesn't even exist."

If Philadelphia was surprised, St. Louis was flabbergasted. No one had even submitted an application to the league for a franchise. But here the plot thickened. James D. Norris and Arthur Wirtz owned the crumbling St. Louis Arena, built in 1929. Norris was an interesting character, to say the least. The NHL owed Norris a favor because "he saved hockey in Chicago," according to author D'Arcy Jenison in his NHL history book.

The son of James E. Norris, who bought the Detroit Red Wings in 1932, James D. Norris was the head of a group, including Wirtz, who purchased the Blackhawks in 1946. The Blackhawks were failures on the ice and at the box office. Norris's financial backing kept the team in business.

In addition to hockey, the younger Norris possessed an intense fascination with the sport of boxing. This was convenient since his father owned New York's Madison Square Garden, hub of the boxing world. Despite a well-known friendship with notorious Mafioso and fight-fixer Paolo Giovanni Carbo, otherwise known as Frankie Carbo, Norris in 1949 managed to get himself named president of the International Boxing Club (IBC) of New York, the dominant force in the world of boxing. Norris's face was familiar in living rooms throughout the United States as he appeared on television at the start of every IBC fight, and there were hundreds of televised bouts in the 1950s.

Norris and brother Bruce wanted to unload the unprofitable St. Louis Arena, and they were looking for a patsy. They found one in Sidney Salomon III, son of Sidney Salomon II, owner of Sidney Salomon Jr. and Associates, an insurance company. Salomon the younger convinced his father to buy the arena from Norris and Wirtz for $4 million.

And so whereas an old building was fine for the NHL if it were located in St. Louis, an old building was insufficient if it were located in St. Paul. It's a shame that Norris and Wirtz didn't own the St. Paul Auditorium. It might have saved Minnesota the trouble of constructing what would be known as the Metropolitan Sports Center in Bloomington.

Chapter 2
MET CENTER

The Metropolitan Sports Center set a record for the speed in which it was constructed. Ground was broken for the construction project on October 3, 1966. The Met Center opened for business on October 21, 1967, for a regular NHL season game between the Minnesota North Stars and the California Seals. The following night, the new facility hosted the American Basketball Association's first game between the Minnesota Muskies and the Kentucky Colonels. The North Stars game attracted 12,951 fans. Attendance at the Muskies game was 8,104. Neither game was a sellout.

Attendance at the North Stars' debut game is in dispute today. The team's general manager and coach, Wren Blair, remembered attendance at closer to nine thousand. Defenseman Mike McMahon placed the number of spectators in the building that night as ranging between seven thousand and eight thousand. Both Blair and McMahon agreed that those in attendance tended to withhold both applause and shouting encouragement for the on-ice efforts of their new team.

Disagreement over the size of the crowd notwithstanding, those who were in attendance seemed to be satisfied that the new building was a respectable hockey arena. Met Center was built in a manner that today is known as "fast-track construction." Construction crews battled six months of Minnesota winter with the goal of creating a major-league facility in the Metropolitan Stadium parking lot.

Groundbreaking ceremonies usually precede actual construction work by a few weeks. This project proved to be an exception. North Stars

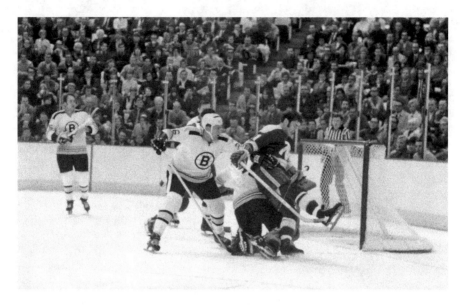

Crowds at early North Stars games were polite and quiet, which was annoying to general manager Wren Blair. *U.S. Hockey Hall of Fame.*

president Walter Bush remarked, "We're starting construction immediately." Photographic evidence shows that instead of a golden shovel, Bush wielded a jackhammer for the benefit of a *St. Paul Pioneer Press* photographer. Next to Bush, Minneapolis mayor Arthur Naftalin swung a pick and, somewhat curiously, St. Paul city clerk Harry Marshall fumbled with a hockey stick. St. Paul mayor Thomas Byrne was a no-show, perhaps in protest to his city losing out with its Auditorium bid.

The Twin Cities were going to be major-league in hockey, just as they were in baseball and football. Many thought this was only right and just. The name "North Stars" came as the result of a fan poll. More significantly, the team, following the lead of the Minnesota Twins and the Minnesota Vikings, would be the Minnesota North Stars, and the state was thought to be hockey crazy. "If you grow up in Minnesota, you put on a pair of skates and go find a rink," high schooler Andy Faust told *Let's Play Hockey* magazine. "It might be a pond or lake somewhere. There are just so many opportunities to get on the ice."

Minnesota is the northernmost state in the union. It is the land of ice and snow—America's Great White North. Like Canadians, Minnesotans encounter ice from October to April. Humans and animals slip and fall on it, autos slide toward ditches on it and kids slap pucks on it. And at the new Metropolitan Sports Center, pipes were laid four inches apart so that a chilled salt solution would freeze water to create an indoor ice surface for the playing of professional hockey. You didn't have to go outside to find ice.

In Los Angeles and Oakland, ice was something you put in your drinks. In Minnesota, ice was a way of life!

Folklore aside, it must be noted that annually enduring potentially hazardous icy conditions does not necessarily result in a passion for hockey. Even in the faraway and somewhat isolated north woods mining area known as the Mesabi Iron Range, all children in the 1950s did not grow up clutching hockey sticks. Myth tends to contradict that notion, and myths surrounding the Iron Range can be strong.

In 1945, only twenty-six high schools in the state had hockey teams, and no one aside from the friends and relatives of the players cared. The Mesabi Iron Range boasted high schools Aurora, Biwabik, Gilbert, Eveleth, Virginia, Mountain Iron, Buhl, Chisholm, Hibbing, Keewatin, Nashwauk, Coloraine and Grand Rapids, and in only one (Eveleth) was hockey the prime winter month attraction. Other schools focused on their winter athletic teams reaching the State High School Basketball Tournament. Eveleth athletes were motivated to advance to St. Paul and the new State High School Hockey Tournament.

Approximately 850 of the participants' friends and relatives gathered at the St. Paul Auditorium to watch Thief River Falls and White Bear Lake face off in the first round of the 1945 hockey tournament. In contrast, opening rounds of the Minnesota State High School Basketball Tournament drew nearly 15,000 to Williams Arena in Minneapolis. Eveleth won that first high school hockey tournament and four in a row from 1948 through 1951, but recognition was slow in coming.

For example, on February 22, 1951, near the fold of the second page of the sports section of the *Hibbing Daily Tribune*, newspaper of record for the Mesabi Iron Range, was a five-sentence item under the heading "State Hockey Tourney Opens." Within the five sentences, it is noted that the Eveleth High School hockey team would be a participant and was "defending champion." No mention was made of the fact that Eveleth was aiming for four consecutive titles or that its star, Johnny Mayasich, held most of the tournament's individual records. The lead items in the *Tribune's* front-page sports section that day were an article outlining the upcoming District 28 High School Basketball Tournament and a piece on college basketball's Madison Square Garden point-shaving scandal. Hockey in 1951 held no prominent place for the editors of the sports department for the *Hibbing Daily Tribune*.

But basketball did, and so did football.

Minnesota first and foremost was a football state. College football put the state on the map. In the 1930s, New York City was the media capital of the world, and New York City knew little and cared less about Minnesota, then considered to be a frozen wasteland. One event, a football game, changed that. The darlings of eastern football in 1934 were the mighty Pittsburgh Panthers. So-called western football powers were granted little respect by eastern newspaper personnel. That changed when the University of Minnesota Gophers traveled to Pittsburgh and defeated the Panthers 13–7, giving birth to a dynasty. The Gophers, under coach Bernie Bierman, won national championships in 1934, 1935, 1936, 1940 and 1941. Thanks to national coverage, everyone knew the location of Minnesota. Two other states, Oklahoma and Nebraska, subsequently used the same football formula to gain national attention to their states.

Where was Minnesota hockey when all this was going on? Hockey was sputtering along with a small but hardcore group of fans and participants.

The hub city for Minnesota hockey is not Eveleth or Roseau or Warrord or Duluth; it always was and always will be the capital city of St. Paul. Although records indicate that organized hockey was being played at the University of Minnesota in Minneapolis a year earlier, the first tournament took place at St. Paul's Aurora outdoor rink in 1896. Two teams from St. Paul faced off with opponents representing Minneapolis and Winnipeg.

The St. Paul Athletic Club took over as kingpins of Minnesota, sponsoring a senior team in 1899. Henceforth, amateur teams wearing the St. Paul Athletic Club banner carried the torch for the sport of hockey in Minnesota. The athletic club wielded tremendous prestige in St. Paul's downtown world in the first quarter of the twentieth century. All aspiring young businessmen and corporate workers strived to seek membership in the club. Joining the club indicated to all that one had "arrived."

By 1914, the St. Paul Athletic Club felt it had the talent, resources and financial backing to join the American Amateur Hockey Association (AAHA), composed of teams from Michigan's Upper Peninsula. Although the Michigan teams were well stocked with Canadians, the St. Paul club won the championship and the first MacNaughton Cup by defeating the team representing Sault Ste. Marie.

The Athletic Club, meanwhile, broke ground for the construction of a new "clubhouse" at Fourth and St. Peter Streets, a building that stands today, albeit under different management.

World War I interrupted play in the AAHA, but the league returned following the armistice. St. Paul lost a three-game championship to Pittsburgh, but four of its players—Frank Goheen, Tony Conroy, Ed Fitzgerald and Cy Weidenborner—were selected to the first U.S. Olympic hockey team. The U.S. team finished second to Canada at the Olympics, held that year in Antwerp.

The AAHA evolved into the U.S. Amateur Hockey Association (USAHA), with three divisions. The 1922 St. Paul team won its division, defeated Eveleth in the playoffs and advanced to the finals, where it lost to Boston three games to two. The following year, St. Paul again advanced to the finals and again lost to a Boston team, this time three games to one.

The heyday of U.S. amateur hockey died in the midst of the Roaring Twenties. The 1925–26 season saw the St. Paul AC competing in the Central Amateur Hockey Association (CAHA) with Duluth, Winnipeg, Sault Ste. Marie, Eveleth-Hibbing and Minneapolis. The team finished with a 16-17-6 record.

Then came an announcement in the *St. Paul Pioneer Press* that due to the "growth of professional hockey in the East," the CAHA was going pro in an attempt to "prevent raids by the National Hockey League upon the playing talent here."

"By 1926," writes hockey historian Roger Godin, "hockey's national landscape had changed, and the age of the amateurs was over." The change agent was the professional NHL and its new American Division, consisting of New York, Boston, Chicago, Pittsburgh and Detroit. St. Paul was left out.

Undaunted, the St. Paul Athletic Club became a charter member of the professional American Hockey Association (AHA) and became known as the St. Paul Saints. Home ice was the State Fair Hippodrome, which "was located on the state fairgrounds near Snelling Avenue," writes Godin. "It had been built in 1906 by the Minnesota State Fair Board for livestock judging, but a natural ice surface of 270 feet by 119 feet was added in 1911. The facility had a capacity of 6,700. It was unheated, but reserved seat holders could go to a warming room during intermissions. There were periodic calls for a more centrally located facility, which came to pass with the addition of natural ice to the downtown St. Paul Auditorium. The first game was played there in January of 1932."

Professional hockey had been played in Michigan's Upper Peninsula since 1904, but took its time migrating to the Twin Cities. That first season (1926–27) saw the Saints in competition with teams representing Minneapolis, Winnipeg, Duluth, Detroit and Chicago. The league halted operation in 1942 due to World War II.

Of particular interest is the St. Paul team of 1935–36. According to Godin, "the team was composed entirely of players with ties to Minnesota. The Saints won the regular-season championship and took St. Louis to five full games before losing the playoff title."

After the war, the league resumed activity under the banner of the United States Hockey Association, and St. Paul was crowned champion following the 1948–49 season. That league subsequently folded in 1951, marking a drought in professional hockey in St. Paul that lasted until the International Hockey League came to town in 1959. The Saints would move to the Central Professional Hockey League before the 1963–64 season. The team's nickname was changed to the Rangers in 1965 to reflect a working agreement with the New York Rangers.

The St. Paul Rangers franchise was transferred to Omaha with the coming of the North Stars. But the St. Paul Saints would soon live again, much to the consternation of the Minnesota North Stars.

Chapter 3
TRAGEDY AND TRIUMPH

The 1967–68 North Stars season is remembered for numerous reasons, not the least of which is the debut of the first Minnesota hockey team in the NHL. Because Met Center was still under construction, the first four October games were played on the road. History will note that the first North Stars goal ever scored was made against the St. Louis Blues by a part-time professional hockey player from Winnipeg, Manitoba, named Bill Masterton.

The Blues game ended in a 2–2 tie, one of fifteen for Minnesota during its inaugural season. (The road warriors finished with no wins, two losses and two ties before the first home game.) However, the name of Masterton is not known today for that first goal. Masterton's name has become synonymous with tragedy.

As a senior at Denver University, Masterton led the Pioneers to the NCAA championship in 1960 and 1961. After two years of professional minor-league hockey, he hung up his skates to pursue a master's degree in engineering at DU. He subsequently was offered a position at the Honeywell Corporation in Minneapolis, which he accepted. There, he worked on the company's end of the Apollo project and eventually became a naturalized U.S. citizen. To keep in shape, he played amateur hockey, including a stint with the U.S. National team. While there, he attracted the attention of the North Stars' general manager, Wren Blair, who was scrambling to find warm bodies for his hockey team. Blair acquired Masterton from the Montreal Canadians, who owned his rights. After a series of team practices, Masterton was given North Stars uniform number 19. He had made the team.

Thirty hours before the last day of his life, Bill Masterton, twenty-nine, was living a dream. He had four goals and eight assists to his credit—not bad for a guy who had not played professionally for four years. It was January 13, 1968. The opponent was the Oakland Seals. In the first period, Masterton advanced the puck past the blue line when he was sandwiched between defensemen Larry Cahan and Ron Harris. He fell awkwardly backward, and the back of his head violently hit the ice. Players on the ice saw this was no ordinary injury. Masterton was bleeding from his mouth, nose and ears. He was not wearing a helmet.

Later, referee Wally Harris said, "He [Masterton] was checked hard, but I'm sure it was not a dirty play."

Masterton was taken by ambulance to Fairview Southdale Hospital, where he was attended to by two neurosurgeons. Unconscious and on life support, Masterton died on January 15 with his wife, two children, brother and parents at his bedside. The North Stars played in Boston that night and lost to the Bruins 9–2.

Masterton remains as the only NHL player to die as the result of injuries incurred when on the ice during the course of a game. Teammate Cesare Maniago recalled that Masterton during his last game complained of a migraine headache, raising speculation that earlier that night he had received a concussion.

The hit that sent Masterton's head crashing to the ice was clean, but Ron Harris remembers it every day: "It bothers you the rest of your life. It wasn't dirty, and it wasn't meant to happen that way. Still, it's very hard because I made that play."

Coach Blair was more specific. "I've never said this to anyone before," he told Randy Starkman of the *Toronto Star*. "I've never thought that [Masterton's death] had anything to do with that hit. I think he had a [preexisting] cerebral brain hemorrhage." The injury had gone undetected by the coach.

Today, most neurosurgeons would agree. Studies have shown that one concussion leaves the brain "vulnerable" to another if the brain isn't immediately given time to heal, according to Mark Fainaru-Wada and Steve Fainaru in *Sports Illustrated* magazine.

Neuropathologist Ann McKee, studying the brains of thirty-four deceased NFL football players, determined that thirty-three had chronic traumatic encephalopathy (CTE), a tau-based disease. Tau is a protein that strangles brain cells.

The fact that Masterton, unlike NFL players, was not wearing a helmet contributed to his death. Toronto neurosurgeon Charles Tatot believes

BILL GOLDSWORTHY

Fans during the early North Stars years have fond memories of Bill Goldsworthy and the "Goldie Shuffle." *U.S. Hockey Hall of Fame.*

Masterton died from "second impact syndrome." When a second concussion happens on the heels of a first, massive brain swelling results.

Masterton was no stranger to helmets. He wore one in college, in amateur hockey and with the U.S. Nationals. But for his thirty-eight games in the NHL, he went bareheaded.

"You were not allowed to wear helmets," teammate J.P. Parise told the *Toronto Star*. "You would be traded if you did. It was a no-no in uncertain terms. You were a yellow belly if you wore a helmet."

Management wanted to see players helmet-less. The argument was that patrons wanted to see players' faces and hairstyles. And, of course, hockey was a macho man's sport in which no one got killed.

Until Masterton.

The North Stars retired number 19, and the number has never been worn by a member of the Dallas Stars.

But it was eleven years before the NHL, moving at its usual glacial pace, mandated the use of helmets for the 1979–80 season. Although the league wishes the Masterton tragedy had never happened, the NHL each year awards the Masterton Trophy to a player who "demonstrates a perseverance, sportsmanship, and dedication" to hockey. This is fitting because it was perseverance that killed Bill Masterton.

Prior to Masterton's last game, the North Stars had to their credit fourteen wins against fifteen losses and eight ties. The team, along with the other five expansion franchises, had been given by the NHL a division of their own, the West Division. This was, of course, ill named since a child of nine could tell you that the existing Chicago and Detroit franchises were west of Philadelphia and Pittsburgh. But simple geography was never an NHL strong suit.

Because the league had been split into two divisions, four of the expansion teams would automatically make the playoffs, with the winner placed in the Stanley Cup finals—quite a prize for a team just starting out. Hockey purists, especially those in Canada, howled in disbelief. Not only was Canada denied a horse in the expansion race, but the new kids on the block had also been handed by the NHL the keys to the Stanley Cup.

Since the league—or any league, for that matter—had never doubled its size by adding six new teams, there were a number of obstacles to overcome, not the least of which was the illusion of parity. After years of operating as a closed society, the doors had been flung open, creating employment in the major league for players and front office people alike. The twelve-team NHL would have a seventy-four-game schedule (instead of seventy) with a "partially interlocking" format. For example, Minnesota would play St. Louis ten times during the course of the regular season and Montreal only four times.

Wren "the Birdman" Blair was given the reins by Walter Bush in hopes that he would create a masterpiece. Blair was hired on May 25, 1966. North Stars owners Bush, Gordon Ritz and Robert McNulty had owned and operated the Minneapolis Bruins, a farm team of the Boston Bruins. Blair had served as coach and general manager of the Minneapolis Bruins, and he was available. From the beginning, it was evident that this would be a Minneapolis, not St. Paul, show.

To be fair, it should be known that Blair was an excellent choice. In Canada, his senior-league teams had twice been presented with the Allan Cup, but Blair was best known in NHL circles as the man who discovered and signed Bobby Orr.

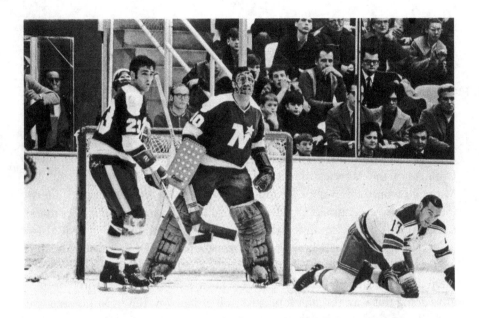

One of the team's early crowd-pleasers was six-foot-three goalie Cesare Maniago (30). *U.S. Hockey Hall of Fame.*

But there were no Bobby Orrs to be found in the NHL expansion draft. Each Original Six team could protect ten skaters and one goaltender. No expansion team could select a "junior" player. A junior player was defined as (1) an eligible player in a junior league or (2) one who was born after May 30, 1946.

The draft order, selected by an earlier drawing, was Los Angeles, Philadelphia, St. Louis, Minnesota, Pittsburgh and Oakland. Goaltenders would be taken first. The Kings selected Terry Sawchuk from Toronto, a future Hall of Famer, and from Boston, the Flyers got Bernie Parent, a goalie who would go on to become a Hall of Fame inductee. St. Louis took Glen Hall, who, up until the draft, had tremendous success as a Chicago Blackhawk. Minnesota's turn came next, and Blair selected Cesare Maniago from the New York Rangers. Maniago had been around.

Born in Trail, British Columbia, on January 13, 1939, Maniago began his career with the St. Michael's Majors in the Ontario Hockey League in 1957. He moved on to the Kitchener-Waterloo Dutchmen in 1959 and, after a stint with the Chatham Maroons, was called up to play 7 games with the Toronto Maple Leafs, where he was 4-2-1. He was claimed by Montreal in the inter-league draft of 1961. He spent time with the Hull-Ottawa Canadiens before being called up by Montreal to play 14 games and go 5-5-4. After that, it was back to the minors, where he spent time with the Quebec Aces, the Spokane Comets, the Buffalo Bisons, the Omaha Knights and the Minneapolis Bruins. It was at the latter city that he performed for Walter Bush and company, going 34-26-7 in 67 games in the City of Lakes.

Maniago was traded to the New York Rangers on June 8, 1965, and played in twenty-eight games, splitting time with the Blue Shirts and the Baltimore Clippers of the American Hockey League. During his stint in Minneapolis, Maniago won the Sawchuk Trophy for fewest goals scored against (ninety-four) and also was named COHL Most Valuable Player. The Rangers made him available in the expansion draft, and Blair nabbed him.

"My first reaction," Maniago said later, "was that I was an outcast, that nobody wanted me. But we had some guys who had been good players. On the teams I had been with before, there always been cliques—three or four guys going this way, three or four guys going that way. But in Minnesota, we had all twenty guys going the same way, together."

A unifying factor was Blair. "We'd all be mad at him almost all of the time," Maniago said. "He'd always be putting you down, knocking everybody. So we all had something in common. The time I spent in Minnesota was likely the best time of all for me."

Chapter 4

SHOOTING STARS

Cesare Maniago was one of several players who made his way to the North Stars roster in 1967 and became a fan favorite. Others were Wayne Connelly, Ray Cullen, Andre Boudrias, Dave Balon, Mike McMahon, Parker MacDonald, Moose Vasko, J.P. Parise and Bill Goldsworthy.

"A surprising amount of talent was available," wrote Jeff Z. Klein and Karl Erik Reif in *Total Hockey*. The expansion draft freed up "plenty of NHL-worthy players who had languished in the minors simply because they had never gotten a real shot in the tiny six-team league."

Klein and Reif went on to explain how the six new NHL teams allowed veteran hockey players to "extend their careers to unprecedented lengths." Players normally relegated to the scrap heap by Original Six franchises were given new life. As the result of the expansion draft, "players could keep on playing through their thirties and sometimes past 40. It was strange to be a fan and see guys out on the ice older than your dad, but it provided a sense of history, a lovingly prolonged view of the torch being passed from one era to the next, and it made the expansion era unique."

Parker MacDonald was eight days short of thirty-four years old when he was claimed by the North Stars from Detroit on June 6, 1967, in the expansion draft. A native of Sydney, Nova Scotia, he began his career in the juniors at the age of seventeen with the Toronto Marlboros and stayed for three seasons. He was given a one-game shot with the Toronto Maple Leafs in 1953 and was subsequently farmed out to the Pittsburgh Hornets of the American Hockey League.

J. P. PARISE

MINNESOTA
NORTH STARS

Today he's better known as Zach Parise's father, but J.P. Parise toiled for the North Stars from 1967 to 1975 and from 1978 to 1979. *U.S. Hockey Hall of Fame.*

Lou Nanne (23) fires a shot at the Montreal net while teammates Danny O'Shea (7) and Danny Grant (21) maneuver. Nanne would later hang up his skates and become the team's GM. *U.S. Hockey Hall of Fame.*

On June 5, 1956, MacDonald was claimed by New York from Toronto in the inter-league draft. His 1956–57 season was spent between the Rangers and the Providence Reds. This began a pattern of minor-league action and in-season call-ups by the Rangers until he was claimed by Detroit in the inter-league draft of 1960. In the 1962–63 season, alternating between center and left wing, he scored thirty-three goals and recorded twenty-eight assists for the Red Wings. He was traded to Boston in May 1965 but was returned to Detroit in December of that same year. In the inaugural year of the North Stars, MacDonald played in sixty-nine games, registering nineteen goals and twenty-three assists.

The team's 9–2 loss at Boston following Bill Masterton's death was followed by a 5–0 drubbing at St. Louis and a 4–2 defeat at home against the Philadelphia Flyers. The losing continued in Toronto on January 20, where the Maple Leafs waltzed to a 5–1 win. From there, Minnesota was able to rattle off 8 wins in 10 games to boost their season record to 22-21-9.

Wren Blair had demonstrated that he could assemble a competitive NHL team. Where he fell short was behind the bench. "He was the classic showman," recalled Lou Nanne in his book *A Passion to Win*. Blair was "flamboyant, demonstrative, and extremely outspoken," according to Nanne. And not much of a strategist.

"He wanted a lot of flair, flashiness, and goal-scoring," Nanne wrote. Blair emphasized offense, and as a result, his team's defense suffered. There were a lot of 6–0, 6–1, 5–0 and 5–1 games that season, and the North Stars lost most of them.

Blair's grandstanding took a toll on his players, most of whom reviled him. Minnesota finished fourth in the new six-team West Division with twenty-seven wins, thirty-two defeats and fifteen ties. The team's sixty-nine points entitled them to a playoff berth, ahead of Pittsburgh with sixty-seven. For contrast between the two divisions (old and new), in the East, Toronto finished with seventy-six points and did not make the playoffs. Fans of the Maple Leafs were livid.

As for the expansion teams, their fans seemed to echo the feelings of Philadelphia defenseman Ed Van Impe, who said, "There are a lot of good hockey players who never got a chance until this year. Until this year, there were only 120 spots open for major-league hockey players. Now it's 240."

The North Stars drew Los Angeles for the first round of the Stanley Cup playoffs. Blair had just signed probably the most recognized hockey player in Minnesota—twenty-six-year-old Louis Vincent Nanne. An All-American at the University of Minnesota (where he was known as the "Ice God"), Nanne was fresh off the U.S. Olympic team when he signed and played his first two games in a North Star uniform.

But what did the Birdman do with the playoffs about to start? By not playing Nanne, he could retain the Ice God's services for three years under NHL rules, not two. So because of a cost-saving gesture, the North Stars entered their first-ever playoff run with their potentially best player out of uniform. Ironically, he was hired to handle broadcasting chores during the playoffs.

Los Angeles held the playoff advantage of home ice, so the first game was played at the "fabulous" Forum on April 4. The Forum was still under construction when the season started, so the Kings had opened on October 14, 1967, at the Long Beach Arena. The first Forum game wasn't played until late December.

The year 1968 was to go down as one of the most tumultuous in U.S. history. On March 31, President Lyndon B. Johnson announced he would neither seek nor accept a nomination for a second term. On the night of the first North Stars–Kings game, Martin Luther King was struck down by an assassin's bullet, touching off riots in Memphis, Birmingham, Jackson, Chicago and Washington, D.C. Later, Senator Robert F. Kennedy would be murdered in Los Angeles.

But at the Forum, it was hockey before a scant crowd of 6,847 spectators. Major-league hockey had yet to take hold in Tinseltown—or in the other five expansion cities, for that matter. The ice sport had developed a cult following and little else.

Minnesota's high-flying, offense-minded hockey style was stonewalled by Los Angeles defenders and crafty goaltender Terry Sawchuk. Meanwhile, the Kings were launching forty shots on Minnesota goalie Cesare Maniago. Two went in. The last by Bill White was the game-winner. The North Stars lost 2–1.

The following day, Blair went screaming to the Los Angeles media, complaining about practice times and schedules. "We were given an 8:00 a.m. practice time this morning in Burbank," he wailed. "That's 40 minutes from our hotel [the Ambassador]. This is bush league. I'm not going to get my players up at six in the morning. No team has been ever treated like this anywhere."

Meanwhile, an intruder broke into Room 68E at the Ambassador and stole the sleeping guest's pants and wallet, which held his cash, driver's license and credit cards. The hotel guest in Room 68E was North Stars assistant general manager John Mariucci. Welcome to the new NHL. The Birdman should have been satisfied that the league had found a practice rink for his team anywhere in Southern California. And Mariucci should be thankful that he packed a second pair of trousers.

The next game was played on a Saturday night, and Sawchuk pitched a 2–0 shutout against the dump-and-chase Stars. This time a date-night crowd of 8,114 wandered into the Forum. The *St. Paul Pioneer Press* refused to hold the presses for the Sunday sports page and led off with a lengthy report on the Minnesota Muskies win over the Pittsburgh Pipers in the second game of the American Basketball Association playoffs. Historians find this interesting because for the following ABA season, the Muskies became the Pipers, a failed attempt to attract larger Minnesota audiences.

Back in Bloomington, before a sparse crowd of 6,797 curiosity-seekers, the North Stars, now down two games to none in the seven-game series, launched an all-out attack on Sawchuk and found themselves down 3–1 in the first period. But Ray Cullen scored to bring Minnesota within a goal, and Mike McMahon's goal tied the game at 3 at the end of the first period.

The much-traveled Parker MacDonald gave the North Stars a 4–3 to open the second period. Then, Wayne Connelly was pulled down on a breakaway and scored on the ensuing penalty shot to make it 5–3. Bill Collins began the scoring in the third period with his second goal of the night, and it was 6–3. The lead looked safe even as the Kings' Ted Irvine scored to make it 6–4, but nervous fans started to panic when Doug Robinson's goal pulled Los Angeles within a goal. Not to worry. Andre Boudrais cemented a 7–5 win with a goal. Minnesota was winning the North Stars way.

In the post-game press conference, Kings head coach Red Kelly muttered, "Some of our guys should have had to pay their way in tonight for what little they did out there."

Game Four at Met Center saw a small uptick in number of spectators with 8,843 passing through the gates. They were rewarded with a 3–2 win. Once again, the North Stars fell behind by two goals at the outset but crept within one when Cullen scored. In the second period, McMahon tied it, and Dave Balon got the game-winning goal. The series was tied at two apiece.

It was back to Los Angeles for Game Five. The Kings blitzed Maniago for a 3–0 lead, and two Connelly goals weren't enough. Los Angeles needed only one more win to take the series.

At Met Center, with their backs to the wall, Minnesota pulled out a thrilling overtime win when Milan Marcetta scored at 9:11. Once again, Minnesota came back from a 3–1 deficit on goals by Bill Goldsworthy and Bob McCord to send the contest into overtime.

The seventh and final game of the Minnesota–Los Angeles series of 1968 took place at the Fabulous Forum, where a surprisingly large crowd of 11,214 had come in from the sunshine to watch the action on the ice. From the second period on, it was no contest as the North Stars attacked the net for five goals and an 8–3 lead. When the horn sounded at game's end, the scoreboard read: Minnesota 9, Los Angeles 4.

The madcap ending to the Kings series entitled the North Stars to face the East Division champion St. Louis Blues for the right to enter the Stanley Cup finals. Of course, the finals had been cheapened by the NHL in that one of the six expansion teams was guaranteed a spot, sort of like granting the Houston Colt .45s an automatic place in the World Series. Be that as it may, here were the North Stars just four wins away from competing for the sporting world's most treasured trophy, the Stanley Cup.

Unfortunately, five of seven games of the series were played at the creaking, ancient St. Louis Arena. How did this happen? An illustration of how little NHL hockey meant locally in those days was the fact that the Met Center ice had not been held open to accommodate the Stanley Cup playoffs. A traveling show, the Ice Capades, had been booked, and the booking was firm. Skates were for ice dancers, not hockey players. That was the order of significance in the Twin Cities metro area, no matter if it cost the local team a run at Lord Stanley's cup. Thus, the North Stars would have only two games on home ice.

In the series opener at St. Louis, Minnesota let a pair of one-goal leads slip and suffered the consequences. In the first period, Marcetta gave the North Stars a 1–0 lead. The Blues answered with a Tim Eccelstone tally to knot the score. Connelly scored in the second period to put Minnesota ahead, but Frank St. Marseille's goal tied it again, 2–2. A goal by Dickie Moore of the Blues made it 3–2, and St. Louis held the lead the rest of the way.

Game Two was at Met Center prior to the heralded arrival of the Ice Capades. Fewer than ten thousand chose to view the hockey event, others perhaps saving their money for tickets to see the figure skaters. Those who did come witnessed an overtime thriller with good old Parker MacDonald scoring on a wrist shot from point-blank range at 9:11 of the extra period. It was Minnesota's first win over the Blues in eight games.

"If I had missed that shot," said MacDonald, "I would have kept on going off the ice in shame."

It was back to St. Louis for the third, fourth and fifth games with the series tied at one. Although outshot 31–21, the North Stars pushed five goals past Blues' netminder Glenn Hall for a 5–1 win. Goldsworthy scored in both the first and second periods. "This gets us back home," chirped the Birdman, pointing out that even if the Blues won the fourth and fifth games, the sixth was guaranteed for the friendly confines of Met Center.

The victory, however, did not stimulate the editors of the *St. Paul Pioneer Press*' sports page. The account of the North Star triumph on foreign ice took second place to a Twins win over the Chicago White Sox.

Blair, meanwhile, proved to be a prophet in that St. Louis did indeed win the next two games of the series, both in overtime. Game Four saw Minnesota take a three-goal lead on tallies by Walt McKechnie, Parise and Connelly, only to squander it. St. Louis came back in the middle of the third period with a goal by Jim Roberts and a pair by Moore. Gary Sabourin scored the game-winner at 1:32 of overtime. With the series now tied, nearly twelve thousand Blues fans crowded into a smoke-filled arena and were rewarded with another win in overtime. This time, it was Bill McCreary who was the overtime hero after taking a pass from Gerry Melynk and slapping home the game-winner at 17:27.

Down in the series three games to two, the North Stars finally returned to Minnesota for Game Six and did not disappoint the record crowd of 15,172 that gathered at Met Center. Maniago was brilliant in the nets and received several standing ovations. Goals by Connelly, Boudrais and Goldsworthy gave Minnesota a 3–0 second-period lead. After Sabourin scored to make it 3–1, the Stars answered with goals by Goldsworthy and Marcetta for a 5–1 victory. Still, the Birdman was not satisfied with the crowd, big as it was. "It seems to me that our fans could make more noise," Blair grumbled.

The decisive seventh game was played on Friday night, May 3, in St. Louis. Amazingly, the game was scoreless well into the third period. Both teams played cautiously, neither wanting to make a mistake in this most-important game. The tension was broken when Cullen screened goalie Hall, allowing McKechnie to score on a thirty-five-foot wrister with 3:11 left to play. It all came apart when Moore tied the game 31 seconds later.

With three minutes left in overtime, Connelly broke free at the red line and went alone toward Hall but was pulled down from behind by Roberts. Even partisan Blues fans thought there would be a penalty shot coming, but to the amazement of all, referee Art Skov did nothing. Skov incredibly did not even call a two-minute minor penalty. Play continued on into a second overtime when Ron Schock took a pass at mid-ice, skated unmolested by the worn-out North Star players and drilled a fifteen-footer past Maniago for the game-winner.

"It was plain to see that Roberts grabbed Wayne from behind," screamed Blair. "That calls for a penalty shot."

"The North Stars," Bill Boni observed in the *St. Paul Pioneer Press*, "were only a breakaway goal away from the Stanley Cup finals.

It would take years for them to get that close again.

Chapter 5
FOOL'S GOLD

The journey to the brink of greatness that culminated with the heartbreak of the overtime loss to St. Louis marked the death of promise for the Minnesota North Stars.

Everything splendid that was accomplished in the playoffs turned out to be fool's gold, and this was apparent in the first two months of the 1968–69 season, one that will live in infamy. On December 1, Minnesota was shut out in the Boston Garden by the Bruins, 4–0, dropping the team's record to 6-12-4. Fans were staying away from Met Center in droves.

A month earlier, Wren Blair had thrown up his hands in despair and ceded the coaching reins to John Muckler, a fine man who previously coached Minnesota's Central Hockey League team in Memphis. Muckler lasted until mid-January, when Blair resumed his coaching duties behind the North Stars' bench, solidifying the theory, popular at the time, of his mercurial nature.

For Muckler, it was too much, too soon. He was not then competent to handle the rigors of NHL coaching. According to Lou Nanne, Muckler's days and nights were filled with "yelling and screaming. It was a lot like fire and brimstone."

If Blair's coaching style was erratic, then Muckler's bordered on the insane. He was to go on to win a Stanley Cup coaching the Edmonton Oilers in 1990, but by then, the brimstone had cooled off considerably. It didn't hurt that, in Edmonton, Muckler "had the best team in the world," Nanne noted.

From December 22, 1968, to January 23, 1969, the North Stars did not win, losing or tying 14 games in the process. The team's record was a laughable 9-29-7.

The lone bright spot was rookie Danny Grant. A native of Frederickton, British Columbia, Grant was traded from Montreal to the North Stars along with Claude Larose for Minnesota's first-round choice in the 1972 amateur draft. He was to spend six seasons with the North Stars but is best remembered for his first.

Grant scored thirty-four goals during the 1968–69 season, tying the all-time NHL rookie scoring record set by Nels Stewart in 1926 and Bernie "Boom Boom" Geoffrion in 1952. In addition, Grant's sixty-five total points set a rookie record, breaking the mark set by Gus Bodnar in 1944.

"Danny was uniquely skilled in a lot of ways," commented Nanne. "You could pass him the puck, and he would take it on his skates, no matter where it was. He made his defensive men look real good the way he could accept a pass. He could put the puck in the corner even when the goalie knew it was going there."

For his efforts, Grant was awarded the Calder Trophy as the NHL's best rookie. It remains one of only two of the league's prestigious regular-season trophies won by a North Stars player in the team's history.

Taking Grant aside, the rest of his team failed to meet expectations. Connelly went from sixty-five points to thirty, and by mid-February he was gone, traded to Detroit for Danny Lawson. Andre Boudrais slipped to thirteen points (from fifty-three) and was sent packing to Chicago for Tom Reid and Bill Orban. Maniago was no better than mediocre, letting in an average of three points per game. On nights when he wasn't in the nets, his replacements, Garry Bauman and Fern Rivard, were held winless.

Parker MacDonald got old and went into coaching, and Nanne turned out to not be the superstar that some anticipated, spending time between the parent club and the minors (Memphis and Cleveland). The season ended with a 3–3 tie with the Kings in Los Angeles. The tie halted a losing streak of six games, including a 7–2 drubbing at Oakland. Minnesota finished last in the NHL in goals scored against the team, 270. No team member who played on a regular basis registered a positive plus/minus rating. Fans grumbled, believing the team was worthless.

It's a funny thing about the NHL. One minute you're down, and the next minute you're up. The equalizer is the playoffs, especially after the Great Expansion. Qualify, and you're a marvelous collection of splendid hockey players. Don't make the playoffs, and your team's a pile of dung. The league in 1969–70 was still allowing the expansion clubs a clear path to the Stanley Cup, and let the critics be damned. For two consecutive seasons, the straight path to the finals had been taken by St. Louis, and for two years in a row,

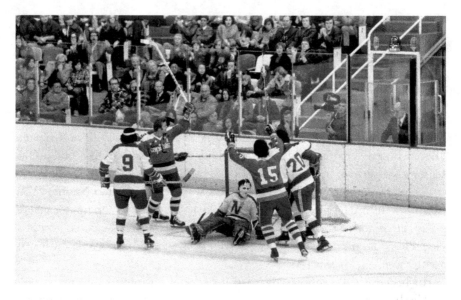

Tommy Williams returned to haunt the North Stars with a goal against Cesare Maniago (sprawling). Other North Stars pictured are Henry Boucha (9) and Tom Reid (20). *Butch Williams collection.*

the Blues had come up winless against Montreal. St. Louis was 0-8 in the Stanley Cup finals series going into the 1969–70 season.

The third year of the existence of the North Stars would see the team's return to respectability via the playoffs, but not before some changes were made.

On May 7, 1969, the North Stars traded for Tommy Williams, a Duluth native who had missed the majority of the previous season with a knee injury suffered on December 13. The popular Williams stabilized Minnesota's offense by serving as centerman on a "production line" in between Parise and Goldsworthy. The trio would finish one, two and three in North Stars' point totals in 1969–70.

Yet that season found the North Stars slogging around with seven wins, nine losses and three ties on December 6, when they upset the defending Stanley Cup Canadians in Montreal, 4–3. The expected momentum change did not happen, however. The North Stars won only once in the next fourteen games. During this time, Blair's on-again, off-again routine was repeated. There was a new twist. This time, the Birdman pointed to the bench and replaced himself with a player, center Charlie Burns. Blair would not, however, grant Burns with a title. Instead, he was to be referred to as "assistant coach."

Minnesota did defeat the Blues at Met Center, 5–2, on January 14 but fell apart, sinking into a losing streak that lasted through February and covered an amazing twenty games. Then, as the month came to a close, it was announced that the North Stars had purchased from Montreal the contract of one Lorne "Gump" Worsley, a once-celebrated NHL goaltender. (Worsley got his nickname from the chinless fictional star of silent movies and newspaper comics, Andy Gump.)

The North Stars had never before had a "name" player in their midst, and fans took notice. The forty-year-old goalie was a perennial all-star and Calder Cup and Vezina Cup winner in the Original Six era with New York and Montreal. Instantly popular throughout the Upper Midwest, the rotund Worsley donned jersey number 1 and made his debut in a 2–2 tie with Philadelphia on March 4, 1970, giving lie to most veteran hockey fans who will tell you that Gump was with the North Stars from the beginning in 1967. Anything is true as long as people believe it.

But one thing is certain: Worsley energized the 1969–70 North Stars. He was in the Minnesota nets for an 8–3 win in Toronto, a 6–3 victory over Pittsburgh and a 4–2 triumph over the Rangers at Madison Square Garden, a North Star first.

The fact remains that at the time of his purchase on February 27, the North Stars were 10-29-18. Minnesota finished the season at 19-35-22, a difference of 9 wins, 6 losses and 4 ties. What is more significant is that the North Stars made the Western Division playoffs, finishing in fourth place ahead of Oakland (22-40-14) and Philadelphia (17-35-24). Ties are important in the NHL.

Born in Montreal on May 14, 1929, the Gumper's career began in 1946, when he tended goal for the Verdun Cyclones. He moved on to the Montreal St. Francis Xavier team and in 1950–51 starred in goal for sixty-four games with the St. Paul Saints, thus establishing a true Minnesota connection.

After minor-league stops in Saskatoon and Edmonton, Worsley was called on to play in fifty games with the New York Rangers at age twenty-three. He was sent back to the minors and spent the entire 1953–54 season in goal at Vancouver. He rejoined the Rangers for the 1954–55 season and stayed with the organization until 1963.

The irascible Worsley was once asked by a New York reporter which team gave him the most trouble in his years with the Broadway Blueshirts, to which he replied, "The Rangers." He escaped New York in a June 1963 deal that sent fellow goaltender Jaques Plante to the Rangers. Both goalies would eventually be enshrined in the Hockey Hall of Fame in Toronto.

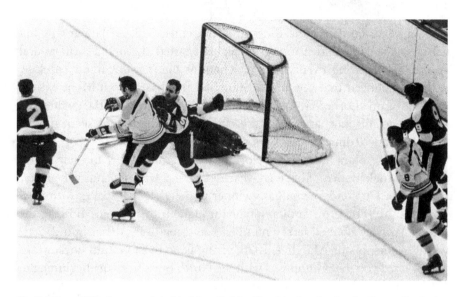

Goalie Gump Worsley sprawls behind Leo Boivin (5) to block a shot by the Boston Bruins' Phil Esposito (7). *U.S. Hockey Hall of Fame.*

Worsley was still with Montreal in 1970 when the North Stars acquired him. Nanne recalled that Gump had an immense fear of flying. In fact, he had turned in his goalie pads after a particularly harrowing flight while a member of the Canadiens, hastening his departure to the North Stars.

On a flight to Pittsburgh to play the Penguins, the plane carrying the North Stars hit an air pocket while dinner was being served, a distressing experience for even the most veteran airline passengers.

"Food flew all over the place," Nanne recalled. After the plane righted itself, an airline representative passed among the passengers. "'We'll have coupons to clean your suits,' and Gump said, 'Suits? What about my shorts?'"

Worsley was in the nets against Philadelphia the final weekend of the 1969–70 season. A win was needed for Minnesota to make the playoffs. Gump and opposing goalie Bernie Parent played flawlessly. The game was a scoreless tie in the third period when Minnesota defenseman Barry Gibbs shot the puck into the Flyers' zone. The eighty-foot shot was on goal and somehow eluded Parent and ended in the net. "I was just trying to get the puck into their end," Gibbs explained later. "Sure, I was aiming at the net, but I never thought it would go in. It's the biggest goal of my life, even if it was a fluke."

The goal held up. Final score: North Stars 1, Flyers 0. The Gumper had pitched a shutout.

The playoffs against the Blues quickly turned into a nightmare. Minnesota lost the first two games in St. Louis, 6–2 and 2–1. Returning home, 14,544 fans watched Goldsworthy score the game-winner in a 4–2 North Stars win. The following night, Maniago shut out the Blues 4–0 to even the series at two.

Coach Burns stuck with the hot hand and named Maniago starter for the crucial sixth game in St. Louis. It was to be one of the many decisions he would regret that season. The Blues peppered the Minnesota net for six goals, and St. Louis won 6–2. Two nights later, on April 16, Red Berenson got the game-winner, and the Blues nailed the coffin shut with a 4–2 victory. Burns was fired that month and replaced by Jack Gordon.

Gordon had spent seventeen years with Cleveland of the AHL as a player, player-coach, coach and general manager and had four championships on his résumé. He was looked on as a stabilizing influence, a man who would be around for a long time. He was neither.

The long line of Gordon's successors would be (in order): Parker MacDonald, Ted Harris, Andre Beaulieu, Lou Nanne, Harry Howell, Glen Sonmor, Murray Oliver, Bill Mahoney, Lorne Henning, Herb Brooks, Pierre Page and Bob Gainey. Only Sonmor, Oliver and Mahoney would leave with winning records.

As for St. Louis, the Blues went on to participate in their third consecutive Stanley Cup finals. This time, while the opponent was different, the results were the same. St. Louis lost four to the Boston Bruins. The Blues' record in the final cup series was 0-12.

Chapter 6
REALIGNMENT

The uproar surrounding the farce that had become the Stanley Cup finals was deafening even before the 1969–70 season. Finally, the National Hockey League said enough was enough and realigned, placing the Original Six team Chicago Blackhawks in the West Division for the following season.

As a further move, after the opening round of the playoffs, the surviving teams would face teams from the opposing division in the second round. One way or another, the NHL had stacked the deck in hopes the change would mean two Original Six teams would meet to decide the winner of the Stanley Cup. And so it came to pass in both 1971 and 1972.

Meanwhile, a pair of Expansion Six teams had been in trouble from the start. The original ownership groups behind the beleaguered Pittsburgh and Oakland franchises had bailed because neither could see things getting better. No one was going out of their way to buy tickets to see either team.

The Penguins seemed destined to meet the same fate that befell another Pittsburgh NHL team. The Pittsburgh hockey Pirates played in the league from 1925 to 1930, finishing the 1929–30 season with only five wins (out of forty-four games).

The new version of the hockey Pirates was having trouble getting six thousand fans into the Civic Arena, which was renamed the Igloo. As a publicity stunt, a real penguin was in the process of being taught how to skate by special trainers on the Igloo ice when it suddenly died. No one could avoid seeing the irony. Approximately 80 percent of Penguins had been sold to a Detroit ownership group, which examined the possibility of moving the team, possibly to Vancouver. Meanwhile, in Oakland, a pair of wealthy brothers, Seymour and Northrup Knox from Buffalo, had committed the funds necessary to temporarily prevent a Seals collapse.

So how did the league react to seeing two of its two prize expansion teams in leaky financial straits? It decided to expand again!

Instead of the logical move of transferring the franchises of a pair of washouts like Oakland and Pittsburgh to, say, Buffalo and Vancouver, the NHL decided to expand to Buffalo and Vancouver and keep in the fold the two duds in the cities Oakland and Pittsburgh. One of those two duds, incidentally, would go on to eventually bite the NHL in the hindquarters.

The NHL raised the price of admission for an expansion club to $6 million.

In exchange for keeping the Seals from folding, the league awarded the Knox boys the Buffalo franchise. The brothers were flush and eagerly paid the $6 million.

There was a problem in Vancouver, however. The franchise applicant, Cyrus McLean, owner of the minor-league Vancouver Canucks, didn't have that kind of money, American or Canadian. It looked like Vancouver would be shut out again—until the North Stars' Walter Bush stepped up and notified the league that he knew of a potential franchise holder.

Tommy Scallen of Minneapolis, owner of, among other things, the Ice Follies and a medical equipment leasing corporation, put up the $6 million and was awarded a franchise in the NHL. At this time, it was perceived that the North Stars were profitable with sound management. In hindsight, one wonders what might have happened to the North Stars if Scallen had purchased the local NHL team instead of taking a flyer at an expansion team—one in Canada, no less.

On the ice under new coach Gordon, the North Stars were an improved team. On November 28, 1970, they defeated the Kings in Los Angeles for their tenth win, against eight losses and three ties. Gordon was a disciplinarian, and he ran a tight ship. Defense was his specialty. "Jack was diligent about defense," Nanne noted. "He really required that from his players, or they didn't play."

The season was marked by the emergence of twenty-six-year-old Bill Goldsworthy as a legitimate NHL star. His trademark "Goldie Shuffle" was known in arenas throughout the league. Used only after scoring when the North Stars were ahead in a game, his ice jig involved employing a locomotive engineer's arm movement with shuffling his skates back and forth several times. Kids loved it, and high schoolers throughout the state imitated it. It brought color to the North Stars.

A native of Waterloo, Ontario, Goldsworthy, at six-foot-one and 190 pounds, was the prototypical Canadian hockey player who proved to be a strong skater and adept puck handler at an early age with the local Siskins Junior B team. Once his potential was analyzed, it was off to Niagara Falls and junior hockey in 1962. His twenty-eight goals in 1965 caught the Boston Bruins' attention, and he was given a two-game look-see.

He spent the 1965–66 season between Boston and the Oklahoma City Blazers. The following year was split between the Bruins, Blazers and Buffalo Bison of the AHL. He was claimed by Minnesota in the expansion draft of 1967. His laconic attitude and propensity to goof off steered the other five expansion clubs away.

"I figured he could make a fresh start with the North Stars," Wren Blair recalled. "I told him I was going to make a good hockey player out of him if it killed us both."

It nearly did.

Nanne remembers the time when Goldsworthy horrified a sold-out Met Center crowd by decking Blair behind the bench in the middle of a home game. As Blair lay flat on his back, trainer Stan Waylett jumped Goldsworthy, and defenseman Tom Reid jumped Waylett.

"Pretty soon," according to Nanne, "we had about six or seven guys piled up on each other" with Goldsworthy and Blair at the bottom of the heap.

They slowly un-piled, and Blair, aware of the crowd and surroundings, informed his player that, between periods, they would chat in the coach's office. There, the two combatants somehow ironed out their differences, and Goldsworthy started the next shift.

Goldsworthy's "chippy" attitude and frequent disinterest in his surroundings were ruining what could be a stellar career. Then something clicked. Perhaps it was a demotion by general manager Wren Blair to the Memphis South Stars in his second NHL season, but he reported to camp in 1969 in the best shape of his life. He reckoned that "80 per cent" of NHL players report out of shape. "I wanted to be in the 20 per cent…Besides, goals are easier to get early in the season than they are late in the year."

That season, Goldsworthy scored thirty-six goals and followed up with thirty-four in 1970–71. He flourished on a line with rookie centerman Jude Drouin and winger Danny Grant. In one stretch of twenty-eight games, Goldsworthy scored an amazing twenty-eight goals. For the season, he and Grant tied for team lead in goals with thirty-four each. "When I got together with Drouin and Grant," Goldsworthy said, "we seemed to click instantly." A poll of NHL players conducted by *Sporting News* placed him at starting right wing for the West Division all-star team.

Goldsworthy recalled that his being sent to Memphis was the "correct move" for him. "At the time, it was a bit difficult…but I didn't have the proper values. Blair's patience with me until I developed was important. I'm happy he stuck with me."

Another North Star on the 1970–71 team was not so lucky. Blair traded the popular Tommy Williams to the California Golden Seals along with Dick Redmond for Ted Hampson and Wayne Muloin on March 7, 1971.

Born in Duluth in 1940, Williams was already a Minnesota legend when Blair acquired him from the Boston Bruins. For years, Williams stood out as the only American to hold down a spot on an NHL roster. He joined Boston in 1961 and became the first U.S.-born skater to play at length in the league since Frankie Brimsek, a native of Eveleth, who had also toiled for the Bruins. Goalie Brimsek is a member of the Hockey Hall of Fame in Toronto.

At nineteen, Williams was on the 1960 Olympic Gold Medal team in Squaw Valley. There, he scored one goal and registered four assists. His best season with Boston was 1967–68, when he scored eighteen goals to go along with thirty-two assists. A serious knee injury in 1968 threatened to end his career, but he came back to score fifty-two assists and fifteen goals with the North Stars in 1970. Williams's brother Butch later played in the NHL.

Tommy Williams's life took a tragic turn when his wife was found dead in November 1970, the victim of an apparent accident. Wren Blair recalled that funeral services were held, and "three or four days later, Tommy returned to the team. He was not able to rehabilitate himself on his own and started drinking rather heavily. All through December and January, he was creating many problems for [coach] Jack Gordon."

Williams and Gordon quarreled frequently over Tommy's tardiness and missed curfews. It didn't help that the crusty Gordon was Canadian and didn't see Williams as America's great gift to hockey.

In what seemed to be a cold response to Williams's problems, the insensitive Gordon suspended him. In today's NHL, constructive steps would be taken to ease such a player through his grief with professional help. Not so in 1970. Assimilate now or suffer the consequences. Organized sport frequently finds itself behind the curve when it comes to sensitivity issues.

Williams's general manager traded him to the highest bidder, which happened to be the California Golden Seals.

"Maybe," Blair wrote in his biography, "Minnesota was the worst place for Tommy to try and turn his life around."

So he traded him. Williams was bitter to the day he died, of a heart attack on February 8, 1992. But he blamed Gordon, not Blair.

Minnesota finished the 1970–71 regular season in fourth place in the new seven-team West Division, one point behind Philadelphia. This entitled the team to once again face Minnesota's now-dreaded rival St. Louis in the playoffs. The tone for the series was set in the opener in St. Louis. The North Stars beat the Blues 3–2 before 18,950 hostile fans, with Drouin getting the game-winning goal.

St. Louis won the next two, including a 3–0 whitewash at Met Center, and Minnesota fans had the feeling of "here we go again." But the North Stars rallied to rattle off three consecutive wins by scores of 2–1, 4–3 and 5–2 to take the series four games to two.

The next opponent was the Montreal Canadiens, fabled in song and story, the most successful franchise in hockey in terms of wins, championship banners, prestige, glory, fame, etc. The series was an example of the new NHL crossover playoff system between western and eastern divisions.

The Canadiens had won the Stanley Cup in 1968 and 1969 and were heavy favorites to appear in the finals in 1971, which they eventually did. But first came the North Stars, seen by the experts as an insect to be leisurely swatted from the path of the Montreal machine. The first game showed that the experts were correct.

The North Stars arrived at the Montreal Forum and were overwhelmed by the tradition, the playoff atmosphere and the Canadiens themselves. Gump Worsley, who had once worn the *rouge et bleu* colors himself, started in goal for Minnesota and wilted under the pressure, allowing seven goals to whiz by him in a 7–2 North Star loss.

All of French Canada had Minnesota dead and buried before the second game of the series. But coach Gordon replaced the befuddled Worsley with Cesare Maniago, another former Canadien netminder. And although Maniago let in three goals, his teammates, led by Nanne, scored six. The series was tied. More importantly, the 6–3 win was the first ever by an Expansion Six team over an Original Six playoff team in the NHL playoffs.

Back on U.S. ice, 15,364 watched Montreal storm back to win the third game of the series, but Minnesota got off the mat for the next one. J.P. Parise scored the game-winner in a 5–2 victory for the North Stars. Once again, the series was tied, and once again, the Montreal Forum proved to be intimating. Now it was Maniago's turn to be a sieve in a 6–1 drubbing.

The series returned to Met Center for Game Six. Gordon stuck with Maniago in the nets, and he responded with a championship-type performance.

Unfortunately, it was not enough.

With six and a half minutes left in the second period, the Canadiens broke a 2–2 tie when Rejean Houle scored rebounding a Henri Richard shot. The 3–2 lead held into the closing minutes of the game, when Gordon pulled Maniago in order to go after Montreal goalie Ken Dryden with six attackers.

With only seconds remaining, Ted Hampson carried the puck across the Canadiens' blue line. He flicked a pass to Drouin, who was checked and unable to get his stick on the puck. The puck hit Drouin's skate and squirted back to Hampson with one second left on the clock. Hampson lifted the puck into the net past the sprawling Dryden.

But the goal light never went on. The green light signifying the game's end cancelled the goal light. The goal did go in, but it was too late. The North Stars screamed at referee Bill Friday, to no avail. Montreal won the series.

Montreal went on to win the Stanley Cup, defeating Chicago in seven games. Order had been restored to the NHL, but not before Minnesota had given a measure of respectability to the Expansion Six.

But a storm was coming.

In June 1971, Delaware attorney Gary Davidson filed articles of incorporation for something called the World Hockey Association (WHA). The WHA resulted from a meeting of three Americans and three Canadians at the exclusive Balboa Bay Club in San Diego. The three Americans were Davidson, Don Regan and Dennis Murphy. The Canadians were Bill Hunter, Ben Hatskin and Scotty Munro. Davidson and Regan were lawyers, and Murphy had been the mayor of Buena Park, California. All three had been closely involved with the founding of the American Basketball Association (ABA) in 1967. The trio had little money but a lot of promotional flair. As for the Canadians, Hunter was president of the Western Canada Hockey League, Hatskin was a self-made millionaire who owned a junior hockey team in Winnipeg and Munro was the owner of the Calgary Centennials.

The outlaw ABA was the logical extension of Branch Rickey's proposed Continental League and the reality of the American Football League (AFL). The 1960s and '70s produced the spawning grounds for new professional leagues to challenge the established order of existing ones.

Davidson announced that his new league would require owners to come up with an outlay of approximately $1.5 million, half of which would be used to entice star NHL players into jumping leagues.

The NHL owners in 1971 operated their own fiefdoms, with their players as their serfs. Each player had a reserve clause in his contract that essentially bound him to a team for life. The NHL operated as a restrictive monopoly, pulling down $50 million per year, while the average hockey player made $25,000 per year.

The league was ripe for plucking but couldn't see it.

That October, Davidson announced that the WHA would operate without a reserve clause.

"We felt [the NHL's] weakness was their arrogance and selfishness," said Murphy. "The NHL thought they had it made and that if they ignored us, we'd go away. They could have knocked us out of the box before we even started if they wanted to. But they didn't, and we didn't go away."

Chapter 7
SAINTS RISE AND FALL

The North Stars, however, could not afford the luxury of ignoring the World Hockey Association. A group of St. Paul investors led by local junkman Lou Kaplan were reigniting the flames of the Minneapolis–St. Paul rivalry that existed prior to 1961 and the arrival of the Minnesota Twins.

An example of the contention between the two cities goes back to the 1950s, when Minneapolis and St. Paul made separate bids for the New York baseball Giants and Cleveland Indians, respectively, and got neither. The two cities eventually reached an agreement when it came to major-league baseball and, subsequently, the birth of the Minnesota Vikings, but a group of St. Paul hockey people remembered that the city was the birthplace of professional hockey in the state. What a shame it was that St. Paul didn't have a hockey team of its own. Gary Davidson and company gave it one.

When the NHL expanded in 1967, the population of Minneapolis and St. Paul together was less than any of the five other expansion cities, and the area was the only one of the group to have a successful big-time university hockey program. Yet the WHA proposed creation of another team in St. Paul. Do the math. There are only so many hockey fans to go around.

St. Paul was targeted because the city, dissatisfied with the ancient St. Paul Auditorium, was constructing a new hockey arena. This piqued Davidson's interest. In fact, the WHA would have placed a franchise in Superior, Wisconsin, had that city been building a sixteen-thousand-seat hockey rink.

The philosophy of "if you build it, people will come" had been tried by the American Basketball Association (ABA) with Met Center and failed

DENNIS HEXTALL

MINNESOTA
NORTH ST☆RS

Winger Dennis Hextall came up with the New York Rangers in 1968 and arrived in Minnesota via a trade with the California Golden Seals. Brother Bryan played with the North Stars in 1975–76. *U.S. Hockey Hall of Fame.*

not once (the Muskies) but twice (the Pipers). The WHA would share the same experience with St. Paul, although it would last longer than the ABA did in Minnesota.

The people who invested in WHA franchises were not all starry-eyed hockey nuts, and Davidson himself admitted he didn't know a hockey puck from a popsicle. "The Canadians," he said, "didn't like it because I didn't know anything about hockey, but over time, we were able to work together."

All investments come with risk. WHA owners were aware that their teams would lose money, perhaps over a period of years. All it took were patience and deep pockets plus the hope that your team would be someday absorbed, like the AFL and ABA, into the senior league. The formula would work for the Winnipeg Jets. A $25,000 investment would be worth $67.5 million in 1996.

But in that first WHA season, the Jets had something no other league team had: Bobby Hull, formerly the face of the Chicago Blackhawks. In 1969, Hull had withheld his services to the Blackhawks in a holdout that stemmed from his dislike of Bill Wirtz, son of team owner Arthur Wirtz. Hull eventually returned to the Blackhawks, but his feelings were bruised. Enter Ben Hatskin, one of the trio of Canadians on the ground floor of the WHA.

Hull's contract with Chicago was up in 1972, and he hadn't heard from the Blackhawks. Meanwhile, Hatskin offered him a $1 million bonus to join him in Winnipeg. The money would come from the coffers of Hatskin and three other WHA owners. Owing to U.S. tax codes, Hull's WHA contract had to be signed in the States. The plane carrying Hull to Winnipeg stopped in Fargo, where the document was signed.

Hull was greeted in Winnipeg by throngs of hockey fans bearing flowers and sweets, and he signed another contract, this one for a $250,000 yearly salary for the next five years, plus $100,000 each for the five years after that. The total was $2.75 million. The NHL would never pay that kind of money to a single player, even if that player was the Golden Jet, Bobby Hull.

Hull was the first player in NHL history to score more than fifty goals, and he did it before the Expansion Six watered down the NHL. He led the Blackhawks to the Stanley Cup in 1961 and was worshiped in the Windy City. He was awarded the Art Ross Trophy in 1960, 1962 and 1966; the Hart Memorial Trophy in 1965 and 1966; and the Lady Byng Trophy in 1965. His career might have peaked prior to 1972, but he was perfect for the WHA and Winnipeg. Was it coincidence that the Golden Jet's new team was named the Winnipeg Jets?

Joining St. Paul and Winnipeg for the first year of the WHA were teams representing Houston, Cleveland, Ottawa, Edmonton, Quebec, New York, Los Angeles, Philadelphia, Boston and Chicago. The last five cities already had an NHL team. By the 1974–75 season, four of those franchises had relocated. The Chicago Cougars remained in existence, as did the Minnesota Fighting Saints.

The Saints were forced to open their inaugural season at the antique St. Paul Auditorium while the new Civic Center was being given its finishing touches by a construction team. The owners of the Saints had spent $60,000 to spruce up the Auditorium, money that, it turns out, they could little afford to spend. A crowd of 7,862 curiosity-seekers showed up to watch the Jets, without Hull, win 4–3. Hull's future with the WHA was delayed in federal court before Judge Leon Higginbotham. The NHL had hired a gaggle of lawyers to stop Hull and others from jumping leagues.

Higginbotham ruled in favor of the WHA and, in his decision, said the NHL was a "bi-national business" whose purpose was "making money." The NHL was a "conspiracy…to maintain a monopolistic position." In other words, the NHL was a monopoly in resistance of trade, and Hull was free to play in the WHA.

According to Don Riley of the *St. Paul Pioneer Press*, the WHA "saved 50 careers and started 100 more."

The crown jewel of that first WHA season was a nationally televised match between the Saints and Hull's Jets in the new Civic Center on January 7, 1973. CBS had agreed to televise the game if the teams would arrange to switch a game originally scheduled for February 13 in St. Paul. Both teams eagerly agreed. In an unrelated move, CBS also announced the sale of the New York Yankees to George Steinbrenner for $10 million.

Modeled after Madison Square Garden, the $19 million Civic Center featured something never seen before or since. The dasher boards consisted of clear acrylic glass. This allowed spectators unparalleled views of the action on the ice. The biggest fans of the clear dasher boards were the thousands of hockey fans who now journeyed to the Civic Center for the annual State High School Hockey Tournament, which, after years of struggle, was now drawing capacity crowds.

Today's Minnesota hockey loyalists are true fans who remember "the days of clear boards at the state tournament," according to sportswriter Kevin Kurtt.

A "soft opening" of the Civic Center was held on the first day of the New Year, 1973, and 11,701 spectators watched the Fighting Saints and Houston Aeros play to a 4–4 tie.

Then, with the national television audience on hand on January 7 at the Civic Center, goalie Jack McCartan, a former Olympic hero, allowed six goals, and the Saints lost 6–2. The Golden Jet had a pair of assists. A less-than-sellout crowd of 13,426 viewed the action in person.

No matter—according to Riley, this "was the beginning of a new era, a wondrous experience for people who claimed the distinction of being the best hockey fans in the world."

Two nights later, only 4,683 of the "best hockey fans in the world" showed up to watch the Saints lose 4–3 to the Los Angeles Sharks in overtime. The management team behind the Saints had somehow come up short when it came to selling season tickets.

Chapter 8
MAYHEM

The North Stars, meanwhile, were doing just fine at the gate with near-capacity crowds attracted to Met Center. Minnesota finished the season with thirty-seven wins, good for third place in the NHL's West Division. Individual standouts included Dennis Hextall, J.P. Parise, Jude Drouin and Danny Grant.

The team's record was good enough to match it with the Philadelphia Flyers in the playoffs. The "Broad Street Bullies" were on the rise. The Flyers had gone from a mediocre expansion team to masters of intimidation in the NHL. The bully nickname came from Philadelphia sportswriter Jack Chevalier after the Flyers had brawled their way to an ugly win over the Atlanta Flames on January 3.

The Flyers' success coincided with a time when more hockey players than ever were claiming major-league status. There were now thirty-two teams in two leagues employing 640 players. The Original Six had six teams and 120 players. There was bound to be a decline in the style of play.

"There is no doubt," wrote Ken Campbell in the *Hockey News*, "that the product was diluted, and it also led to marginal players having a much bigger mark on the game."

Fans were now seeing a game that was less pure when compared to the graceful style employed by the Canadiens and the Maple Leafs of the 1950s. Unfortunately, the majority of fans watching those teams in person or on television lived in Canada. Most Americans had never seen "old-time hockey."

Expansion and the World Hockey Association gave jobs to less talented, rowdy players unafraid to use their fists. *U.S. Hockey Hall of Fame.*

Montreal Hall of Fame goaltender Ken Dryden (29) said the Philadelphia Flyers "showed contempt for everyone and everything." *Butch Williams collection.*

For better or worse, fighting has always existed as part of the sport, but in the '50s, it was deemed necessary only to protect star players from cheap shots. Unfortunately, newspaper cameramen concentrated on shooting the occasional fisticuffs between players, resulting in wire services picking up their photos for display throughout the United States. The truth is NHL players of that era did not go out of their way to start fights. Two leagues and 640 players meant a lot of them had no business playing major-league hockey. In order to survive, some became brawlers intent on "gooning it up."

The Philadelphia Flyers, Campbell wrote, "were an up-and-coming team that had some impressive top-end talent but also a roster that was chock full of lesser talents who could intimidate. Sensing he could gain a competitive advantage, coach Fred Shero went out to indelibly change the complexion of the game with that team."

It was like spitting on the *Mona Lisa*. Shero and his boys didn't care. "They were bullies," observed Montreal goaltender Ken Dryden. "They showed contempt for everyone and everything. They took on the league, the referees, and teams…They searched for weakness, found it, trampled it, then preened with their cock-of-the-walk swagger."

The underdog North Stars skated into the Philadelphia Spectrum on April 4, and goalie Cesare Maniago shut out the Flyers 3–0 on goals by Hextall, Dennis O'Brien and Drouin. Jack Gordon was elated. "Winning the first game was a big boost for us," he said.

The same night, the Fighting Saints were engaged in a special one-game playoff with the Alberta Oilers of Edmonton at the Corral building in Calgary (Edmonton's home ice being otherwise occupied). Minnesota won 4–2 on goals by future North Star Mike Antonovich and Bill Young before 6,445 at the Calgary Corral. The Saints thus won the right to travel to Winnipeg and face Bobby Hull in the playoffs.

The following night, the Broad Street Bullies showed up in full force at the Spectrum. In the first period, Bill Barber of the Flyers took on O'Brien, while Parise fought off Andre Dupont. The Barber fight carried over to the penalty box, where O'Brien was seen using a nearby photographer's camera and unipod as a weapon in an attempt to smash Barber's skull. Fortunately, cooler heads prevailed.

The North Stars, however, lost their poise and rolled over to the Flyers, losing 4–1. Barber had one of the goals.

The next night, in Winnipeg, the Jets top line of Hull, Chris Bordeleau and Norm Beaudin produced a pair of goals in the final two minutes for a 3–1 win.

At Met Center on April 7, before 15,647, Maniago was once again brilliant in the nets, pitching his second straight playoff shutout. A typical penalty-marred game resulted in one team or the other on the power play, but only one team, Minnesota, profited. Goals by Hextall, Gibbs and Nanne put the game away for the Stars, and Minnesota was up two games to one. It was to be their last hurrah of the 1970s.

On April 8, both the Saints and the North Stars were engaged in playoff games, and for both, the results were the same. Goals by Bordeleau and Hull were too much for the Saints, and the team lost in Winnipeg.

And home ice was no advantage for the North Stars. Philadelphia coach Shero told his team to forget about fighting and concentrate on rebound shots. "We went after second shots, and it paid off," he said.

Bobby Clarke scored on a rebounder in the first period, and it proved to be all the Flyers needed as goalie Doug Favell stopped all thirty-one shots aimed at him. The North Stars lost 3–0, and the series moved back to Philadelphia tied.

Minnesota had no better luck at the Spectrum. After a Goldsworthy goal sent the game into overtime, Gary Dornhoefer tallied the winner. "Unfortunately, overtime games are like that," philosophized Gordon.

That same night, the Fighting Saints returned to their St. Paul home down two games to none and emerged victorious over the Jets, 6–4, with Winnipeg native Jimmy Johnson scoring the game-winner in the third period. The game provided St. Paulites with a chance to come out and show their support for the hometown team, but apparently someone failed to get the word out in the hockey capital of Minnesota. Only 5,151 showed up. Winnipeg then took a 3-1 series advantage in overtime on April 11.

The Flyers disposed of the North Stars on home ice to end the series and advance. Flavell stopped thirty-eight North Stars shots. Ross Lonsberry scored two goals, and to add to Minnesota's mortification, even the Flyers' notorious goon Dave "the Hammer" Schultz scored a goal on Maniago.

The Jets-Saints series moved back to Winnipeg on April 15. Fans of the Fighting Saints could console themselves with the knowledge that their team lasted longer in the playoffs than did the North Stars. Such joy, however, did not last, as coach Glen Sonmor was forced to yank goalie Lefty Curran in an 8–5 drubbing. Beaudin got the hat trick and added two assists for the Jets, who took the series 4-1. "We were scrapping to the end," said Sonmor. "Overall, I think we had a very good season."

What Sonmor said publicly, he did not echo privately. He had assembled a team consisting of smooth skaters and popular Minnesota natives such as

McCartan, Antonovich, Curran, Dick Paradise, Billy Klatt, Len Lilyholm, Frank Sanders, Craig Falkman and Keith "Huffer" Christiansen. In addition, he brought in former North Stars Wayne Connelly, Mike McMahon and Ted Hampson. The team combined speed with a skilled passing game.

So why did so few fans show up for the playoffs, especially when the opponent was the Golden Jet, the man who made the WHA legit? To Sonmor and the team's owners—Lou Kaplan, Frank Marzitelli, Len Vannelli and John Massaff—the answer was simple: goon it up.

A fan survey revealed few purists among those polled. A prime attraction, the survey showed, would be at least one fight per game. According to Ed Willes in his book *Rebel League*, Sonmor discovered he had "grossly misread the St. Paul market." The market wanted blood.

From the summer of 1973 to the end of their days as a franchise, the Fighting Saints put the emphasis on the fighting part of their nickname. Sonmor stepped down as coach to concentrate on the general manager portion of his job and assembled a menagerie of thugs and goons. Along the way, he was indirectly responsible for the creation of one of the best sports motion pictures ever and probably the greatest hockey movie of all time.

Slap Shot, starring Paul Newman, was born out of the Fighting Saints' working relationship with a minor-league hockey team in Johnstown, Pennsylvania, once the site of a devastating flood. General manager of the Johnstown Jets was John Mitchell, Sonmor's father-in-law.

On the Jets' roster was an American-born, college-educated player named Ned Dowd. Dowd had a sister, Nancy, a screenwriter who would later receive an Academy Award. Nancy hung out with Ned and his screwball teammates and was inspired to write a screenplay about Ned's experiences. That screenplay was for the movie *Slap Shot*.

The movie became a classic as soon as the great Paul Newman signed on. While the film ostensibly is about the struggles of Ned Dowd (Ned Braden in the movie), it is Newman's film from his first scene. His Reg Dunlop, based on John Brophy, a minor-league player-coach, carries the picture and makes us care about the story line, however improbable it may seem.

Of course, everyone remembers the notorious Hanson brothers. What few know is that they really were the Carlson brothers, proud natives of Virginia, Minnesota, Queen City of the Mesabi Iron Range. In real life, the Carlson brothers terrorized the North American Hockey League (NAHL) by bumping, brawling and boarding the opposition. Graceful puck handling was not required of them. When it came to making the movie, the producers decided they should play themselves.

In his minor-league days, Jack Carlson of Virginia, Minnesota, was unintentionally part of the inspiration for key characters in the movie *Slap Shot*. He later played for the North Stars. *Walt Berry photo.*

The Saints' Sonmor fancied best Jack Carlson, eldest of the scrappy clan, and promoted him to the parent team, making him ineligible to play himself in the movie. Dave Hanson, a left-handed defenseman from Cumberland, Wisconsin, stepped in to Jack's role, and the Carlson brothers became the Hanson brothers.

Other names were changed to protect the guilty. John Mitchell became McGrath (played by the ever-popular Newman foil Strother Martin), goalie Louis Levasseur became Denis Lemieux and the Johnstown Jets became the Charlestown Chiefs.

History records that the Carlsons really wore glasses because they couldn't afford the price of contact lenses. The black tape was to hold the glasses' rims, frequently broken, together. The taped glasses and Chiefs jerseys are still being worn by kids on Halloween in the Upper Midwest.

Harry Neale, who succeeded Sonmor as Fighting Saints coach, had a chance to see the real Carlson brothers in action during a scouting trip to Johnstown. Neale observed "three guys wearing black safety glasses and terrorizing the other team…Two of the three end up in the stands fighting with fans…They got arrested, and I had to go post $200 for their bail."

Neale didn't realize it at the time that these man-children, with their disdain for hockey's aesthetics and their propensity to play with slot cars, were perfect for the silver screen.

All three Carlsons wound up playing some with the Fighting Saints, and Jack eventually became a North Star. Levasseur played in goal for thirty-four Saints games and later with Edmonton, New England and Quebec. Records reveal that he actually started one game with the North Stars in his career but let in seven goals. However, it was another *Slap Shot* hockey villain, the fictional Ogie Oglethorpe, played by Ned Dowd, who gained the movie's most attention.

Ogie Oglethorpe was based on Bill "Harpo" Goldthorpe, perhaps the most notorious thug in the history of hockey. In the movie, he was the most-feared of Chiefs' opponents. In real life, he was once a Minnesota Fighting Saint.

"There were stories," said Dave Hanson, "that he was assigned a police escort to the games. He was kind of like a Doberman. You never knew if he would turn on you."

With Syracuse in the NAHL, Goldthorpe accumulated 287 penalty minutes in only fifty-four games.

By the time Goldthorpe arrived in St. Paul, Sonmor had already acquired enforcer Gord Gallant and a circus full of miscreants and troublemakers. Publicity photos showed Goldthorpe and Gallant together, fists upraised, ready to take on all comers.

Former WHA player Paul Stewart remembered that, when in the midst of a mêlée, Goldthorpe, in full Doberman mode, bit him. Stewart recalled that had to have a tetanus shot.

Goldthorpe was remembered for attacking Mr. Hockey, Gordie Howe. "You can't play forever, old man," he screamed. "When you retire, I'm going after your kids."

In one game, Goldthorpe was assigned to check Houston's John Schella but, in the process, drew a penalty. When the penalty expired, he made a beeline at Schella, and a fight ensued. After the fight subsided, the referees sent both players to the penalty box, and referee Bill Friday handed Goldthorpe an extra two-minute penalty. He had left the penalty box without his stick and gloves.

Goldthorpe and Gallant were followed in St. Paul by Kirk Brackenbury, a winger from Kapuskasing, Ontario, and the Long Island Cougars of the NAHL, where he had drawn 194 minutes in penalties in forty-five games. Brackenbury, who was quickly put on a line with fighters Jack Carlson and former Minnesota Gopher Bill Butters, was known for putting into practice in the WHA what the Hanson brothers did in *Slap Shot*—putting on "the foil." Brackenbury wrapped his fists in aluminum foil and then covered the aluminum foil with tape before donning his gloves. It put more power in his punches.

Those who followed their Fighting Saints loved the mayhem. Unfortunately, there were too few of those fans. The team was able to siphon off a portion of the North Stars' crowds, but that, too, was not enough to

One of Glen Sonmor's unsuccessful schemes was to sign Bobby Orr (left) to a Minnesota Fighting Saints contract. *Butch Williams collection.*

provide a profit. After a disappointing first season at the gate, the Saints averaged 6,854 per game at the Civic Center the following year.

The third year, Civic Center crowds averaged 8,410. Something more was needed, and Sonmor attempted to sign Boston's Bobby Orr for a $1 million bonus plus a salary three times that of Bobby Hull's but failed. He did succeed, however, in driving up the price for Orr in Boston, and Orr profited by it. Orr's story was becoming a familiar one, with NHL players using the WHA as leverage for better contacts.

NHL great Stan Mikita of the Blackhawks, who, unlike Bobby Hull, stayed in Chicago, said every NHL player should "bow down to [Hull], on their knees. He did more for us than any player in history. Nobody else could have done it."

Most NHL teams, including the North Stars, could only turn a profit if they made the playoffs, and the North Stars weren't making the playoffs.

In retrospect, if Orr had chosen the Fighting Saints, he would have never seen the $1 million bonus. The team simply did not have the money. The few dollars the Saints did have in the bank ran out in 1976. By then, the WHA had franchises in Houston, Indianapolis, Phoenix, Calgary,

Toronto, Cleveland, San Diego, Cincinnati, Hartford, Quebec, Edmonton and Winnipeg. The latter four eventually would be absorbed into the NHL, and three of them would be relocated. Only the Edmonton Oilers have survived intact.

Saints players sensed early on in the 1975–76 season that ownership, now headed by Wayne Belisle, was in trouble. Payrolls weren't being met, and players were threatening to seize gate receipts or strike.

A critical juncture involved a lengthy mid-season road trip and meal money. Belisle was informed by Sonmor and Neale that the players needed meal money for the trip, or they wouldn't go. Belisle was strapped, so he wandered from bar to bar in downtown St. Paul with a brown paper bag, begging for patrons to fill it to save professional hockey in the capital city. Surprisingly, they did.

Belisle arrived with his sackful of cash at the gate just before the plane was to depart and handed it to Neale. The team boarded while Sonmor and Neale opened the bag and counted out the twenties, tens, fives and ones donated by public-spirited St. Paul bar patrons. The plane crew thought Belisle had stuck up a bank.

Chapter 9
THE GUNDS

The story by Parton Keese on page B14 of the June 14, 1978 *New York Times* read, "The Cleveland Barons and the Minnesota North Stars have agreed to combine their starting teams for the 1977–78 season, the National Hockey League's Board of Governors announced today. As a result, the NHL will be reduced to 17 teams."

What? Preposterous! How could something so wacky happen in a so-called major professional sports league?

Nothing remotely like this had previously taken place in the NHL. Merging two pro teams to form one? Not in times of world peace. Not even in the salad days of the National Basketball Association, when teams such as the Baltimore Bullets, Washington Capitals and Indianapolis Olympians folded like cheap tents, had something like this occurred. Those teams just went away, carrying with them a semblance of dignity.

But the NHL had to be different. By fusing the Barons with the North Stars (the Baron Stars?), the NHL exposed a bush-league foundation. Imagine the Tampa Bay Rays merging with the Oakland Athletics.

The closest a major league would come to duplicating a stunt like this was when Major League Baseball threatened to dissolve the Expos and Twins. And this, it should be noted, was an empty threat that had no traction.

But not only did the NHL, on June 12, 1978, threaten to combine two teams, it actually went ahead and did it! Four days later, some sixty-five players who had previously been affiliated with one of two NHL teams now belonged to a single entity owned by brothers George and Gordon Gund.

According to Pat Thompson of the *St. Paul Pioneer Press*, NHL owners at the meeting on June 12 were "astounded by a motion from George Gund [co-owner with his brother of the Cleveland Barons]." Gund proposed to have the North Stars "consume the struggling franchise" that was Cleveland. For $12 million plus payment of outstanding debt, he and his brother would then take control of the North Stars.

And the board of governors swallowed this byzantine plan hook, line and sinker. Not all were happy about it, though.

The deal had been finalized in a literally smoke-filled room, according to Lou Nanne, who had been named the North Stars' general manager that February. As he left for the NHL meetings in Montreal in June, Nanne says he "didn't know anything" about a merger. Once at the headquarters hotel, Nanne was approached by North Stars owners Gordon Ritz and Robert McNulty and pulled into a room, where he was introduced to the notorious Gund brothers.

"The room was filled with cigar smoke," Nanne recalled. He was introduced to George and Gordon Gund, the latter of whom was blind, which seemed to make him impervious to his brother's cigar smoke. The brothers' attorney, however, stationed himself in the bathroom. "He was in the bathroom because he couldn't stand smoke," Nanne said. "So he would open and close the door" at key moments.

"What am I getting into here?" Nanne wondered. Ritz filled him on the deal that would make the Gunds his new bosses and told him to drop in on the NHL board meeting being held in another room.

According to Nanne in the book *Minnesota North Stars* by Bob Showers, he arrived in time to hear Sammy Pollock, general manager of the Montreal Canadiens, say of the proposed merger, "Gentlemen, if you got one bag of shit and put it together with another bag of shit, all you get is a bigger bag of shit."

In 1978, the North Stars had finished last in the Smythe Division with a record of 18 wins, 53 losses, and 9 ties. The Cleveland Barons' 1977–78 season's record, under the Gunds, was 22-45-13, good for last place in the Adams Division. The brothers claimed losses totaling $3.5 million.

The Gunds came up with the idea of merging with the struggling Washington franchise, but that notion was nixed by commissioner John Ziegler, who thought the NHL board wouldn't go for it.

Ziegler could, however, sell a Barons–North Stars merger to the board. After all, the North Stars had lost an estimated $10 million over the previous five years. Season ticket sales had gone from twelve thousand to under five thousand.

The Fighting Saints were dead, but they had nearly dragged the North Stars to the grave with them. "Two pro teams," wrote historian D'Arcy Jenish, "playing in two rinks had been chasing a limited pool of fans" in the Twin Cities.

A Harvard graduate, Gordon Gund had played hockey for the Crimson and served in the U.S. Navy. He began losing his eyesight to retinitis pigmentosa, and by 1970, he was totally blind. He and his brother George were members of one of Cleveland's most prominent families. The family had parlayed a brewing business into extensive real estate and financial holdings.

Brother George had established a home in the Bay Area and had held a minority interest in the troubled California Golden Seals NHL franchise. The Seals were doomed from the start, a product of the NHL's insistence on a presence in the San Francisco market. When the area was awarded an Expansion Six franchise, an unconfirmed rumor indicated that in order to obtain a national TV contract, the NHL had to produce a team in San Francisco. The fabled Cow Palace was the natural site, as minor-league teams had drawn well there. But the league insisted the expansion team had to make the Oakland Alameda Coliseum its home, immediately sounding the death knell for the franchise. Gertrude Stein remarked when asked her opinion of Oakland, "There is no there, there." In 1967, Oakland was a place where no respectable San Franciscan would consider visiting.

Two ownership groups had vied for the Bay Area expansion franchise. One was headed by Mel Swig, who owned the WHL San Francisco Seals. The other was an investment group fronted by Barry Van Gerbig, twenty-nine, who was a goalie on the 1962 U.S. National team. The NHL selected Van Gerbig, whose investment group consisted of fifty members, including crooner Bing Crosby. According to Alan Bass in his book *The Great Expansion*, "Though Swig seemed to be the better choice from a financial standpoint, there was much controversy surrounding him, with rumors pointing to the league's feelings toward his Jewish heritage."

Four years of failure at the gate and on the ice in Oakland eventually led to the purchase of the Seals by goofy Charlie Finley, owner of the Oakland Athletics, the team that played baseball next door. Finley, long a thorn in the side of organized baseball's upper echelons, picked up the Seals for $4.5 million in 1970 and immediately commenced to "Finleyize" the team. He changed the name of the team to the California Golden Seals. The team colors would be green and gold, reflecting the owner's obsession with those two colors in all things Finley. And he mandated white skates for all team members. (The Athletics were known throughout baseball for their distinctive white shoes.)

Finley's lack of knowledge of ice sports was evident when it came to skates. Any child of five who grows up where ponds freeze know that white skates are "figure skates" worn by girls. After the Golden Seals had been greeted with gales of laughter from fans, opponents and officials, the team's general manager convinced Finley to switch to green-and-gold skates.

Then came the World Hockey Association and the slow death of the Seals. The under-financed Finley lost five top players to the WHA, and the team finished sixth in the seven-team West Division in 1972. The following season, the team occupied last place. The Seals had become an embarrassment to the league and the Bay Area.

Finley tried to dump the team, but no one wanted to buy it. The NHL was forced to take control of the franchise in February 1974. The league finally found a buyer in Mel Swig, the man the NHL had initially rejected. Swig, a San Franciscan who found Oakland repugnant, hoped his city would build him a new arena, but after an unfavorable mayoral election, all bets were off. Swig wanted out, and the NHL agreed. Minority owner George Gund convinced Swig to sell and move the California Golden Seals to Cleveland, where they would be known as the Barons.

But George Gund's heart remained in San Francisco.

Chapter 10
REBIRTH

It needs to be reported that the unorthodox merger of two NHL teams, no matter how wacky, energized Minnesota's professional hockey market. According to the *Hockey News*, the "amalgamation of the North Stars and the Barons had one immediate effect. The switchboard was overloaded with calls from across the state. North Stars executives were beaming…not in five years had the public shown as much interest."

Still, the North Stars of 1977–78 were a bad team, and while the merged Minnesota/Cleveland franchise managed ten more wins in the following season, the team again failed to make the playoffs.

"I coached for the last month and one-half of the 1977–78 season," Nanne recalled. He succeeded Andre Bealieu, who, in turn, had succeeded Ted Harris that season. "I knew I'd coach until the end of the season and then hire a coach. I had coached the University of Minnesota freshman team for four years and some Olympic development leagues for four or five years, and I knew I never wanted to be a coach."

Nanne's record as coach of the North Stars was 7-18-4.

"When I first started in the role of general manager," Nanne wrote in his autobiography, "I can honestly say I was not very well prepared to do the job. I had been a player, and this was very different for me. One day I was a player just like everyone else on the team, and the next day I was the boss."

One of Nanne's first duties was to dump popular defenseman Doug Hicks, trading him to Chicago for goalie Eddie Mio, who never played a minute for the North Stars. Hicks was a pal who car-pooled with Nanne.

"Unfortunately," Nanne observed, "Doug made a great deal of money, and our budget was very tight."

Welcome to the new NHL.

By the 1979–80 season, the North Stars had been molded into a playoff contender. The team with finished the season in third place in the Adams Division with thirty-six wins and was destined to face the twin pillars of the NHL—Toronto and Montreal—in the Stanley Cup playoffs.

Toronto came first. In its first playoff win since 1973, Minnesota bombarded goalie Jire Crha with sixty-one shots en route to a 6–3 victory. What was notable about the match was Toronto's uncharacteristic resort to hooliganism. "They started hitting guys from behind," complained right wing Ron Zanussi of the North Stars. "They showed us no-guts hockey. They wanted to start gooning it up."

Thus the fall from grace of one of hockey's oldest institutions. The age of the goons was now complete. Howard Ballard, the flamboyant owner of the Maple Leafs, was on record as noting that if winger Inge Hammerstrom went into a rink's corners with his pockets full of eggs, he would not break a single one. Ballard wanted broken eggs, lots of them.

The Toronto game played second fiddle in the sports pages the following day to the news that Herb Brooks was stepping down from his post as head coach of the Minnesota hockey Gophers, to be succeeded by assistant Brad Buetow. Immediately, speculation was raised about Brooks taking over as coach of the North Stars. Be careful of what you wish.

The second game of the Toronto series was at Met Center before 15,408 spectators, and the result was the same. Toronto's goons were blown away by a barrage of seven North Stars goals on forty-three on-net shots. Al MacAdam had a pair of goals in the 7–2 route.

"We are a tired team," lamented Toronto's Borje Salming.

The series moved on to Maple Leaf Gardens, where the North Stars put Toronto out of its misery, 4–3, in overtime. Just thirty-two seconds into the extra period, MacAdam scored on a rebound shot past goalie Crha, and the Maple Leafs were cooked. Afterward, an enraged Ballard accused his team of packing their golf gear as part of a new pre-game ritual rather than thinking about playing hockey.

Toronto last played in the Stanley Cup final game in 1967. The Maple Leafs have yet to return to that lofty height.

The Montreal series was next for the North Stars. The memory of the 1971 playoff defeat lingered in the minds of hockey die-hards in the Land of 10,000 Lakes. Here, at last, was the chance for revenge in a playoff setting.

It didn't take long. Before 15,576 hockey fanatics at the Montreal Forum, goaltender Gilles Meloche made twenty-three saves in a 3–0 Minnesota win. The game was scoreless until the third period, when Kent-Erik Andersson scored. Goals by Payne and MacAdam followed. The Canadiens had previously gone twenty-four games without losing.

Montreal fans are quick to point out that Les Habitants were without the peerless Guy LaFleur, the most shining star in all of French Canada. Before the game, Minnesota coach Glen Sonmor was skeptical about LaFleur's reported knee injury. "We take all injury reports with a grain of salt," grumbled the coach. But LaFleur did not play that night or in the rest of the games in the series.

The North Stars amazed the hockey world by winning the next game at the Forum, 4–1, to take a two-game lead going into the home ice of Met Center. The Canadiens were booed in their own building. Meloche made forty stops, and Payne got a pair of goals, but the game was shoved off the Twin Cities sports page with the news that the Vikings had traded their all-time leading rusher, Chuck Foreman, to the New England Patriots. Viking news was important. The football team was fast approaching a popularity that currently exceeds that of all pro sports combined (plus those at the university) in the Gopher State.

Nevertheless, 15,820 loyalists turned out on April 19, 1980, and watched the North Stars lay a giant egg, losing 5–0 to Montreal. Norm Dupont got the first goal in the first period off Meloche, and that was all the Canadiens needed. Pierre LaRouche, Montreal centerman, explained the strategy: "We score first and break their balloon. We win Game 3, and we win the series."

LaRouche was looking like a prophet in Game Four. The Stars played dead and lost again. This time it was 5–1, with Steve Shutt getting the game-winning goal. Now it was the Minnesota fans' turn to boo.

"When you wear the Montreal uniform day after day," said coach Claude Ruel, "the pressure is on you. It's best two of three now."

The return to Canada seemed to give Montreal extra strength. The North Stars kept Game Five close until a third-period shorthanded goal by Doug Jarvis gave the home team a 3–2 lead. That goal opened the floodgates for Montreal, and the Canadiens went on to win 6–2. "We win," said Ivon Lambert of Montreal, "because we work as hard as we can."

News of the Twins opener against the Angels took precedence over hockey news on the local sports pages. It was noted, however, that the North Stars were one game away from playoff elimination.

The North Stars faced off against Philadelphia's Broad Street Bullies in playoff series in 1973 and 1980 and lost them both. *U.S. Hockey Hall of Fame.*

That didn't happen. Goals by Steve Christoff, Andersson, Paul Schmyr, Bobby Smith and Glen Sharpley in the second period surprised Les Canadiens. Minnesota won this one 5–2. "When we had our backs to the wall," remarked Shmyr, "we showed our true colors. Anything can happen now."

And anything did. Montreal had not lost a Stanley Cup quarterfinal game since 1964. But they lost this one. MacAdam scored with eighty-six seconds remaining in regulation before 17,465 stunned fans in the Forum to win 3–2. The North Stars advanced, and the Canadiens packed their golf gear. "Beating Toronto gave us confidence," MacAdam revealed after the game.

That confidence carried over to the first period of the first game of the next round, where Minnesota drew the Broad Street Bullies in Philadelphia. In a wild game that saw seven goals scored in the first period, including five within three minutes and twenty seconds, the North Stars trailed 4–3.

Steve Christoff opened the scoring to make it 1–0 North Stars, only to see Philadelphia's Al Hill score to tie the game. Christoff scored again, and after a Schmyr goal, it was 3–1. The Flyers came back on two goals by Kenny "the Rat" Linseman and one by St. Paul–born Tom Gorence to give Philadelphia a 4–3 lead. This was all in the first period alone.

In the second period, Denver-born Mike Eaves of the Stars lit the goal light for a 4–4 tie, and later, Payne got the game-winner. Payne later added an insurance goal. Sonmor was ebullient. "We have a bunch of guys with a great deal of faith," he screamed in the locker room afterward. "There is a good possibility we could head home two games up."

That possibility was shattered on May 1 when St. Paul's own Paul Holmgren led his band of bullies to a 7–0 smashing of the Stars at the Spectrum.

Minnesota drew crowds of 15,706 and 15,650 to the next two Stanley Cup semifinal matches at Met Center, indicating that a strong following had been established. Unfortunately, Minnesota continued the long statewide tradition of sports disappointments. The North Stars lost both home games of the series, 5–3 and 3–2.

The final game in Philadelphia went no better, as the Broad Street Bullies blitzed Minnesota 7–3.

The Flyers went on to lose to the New York Islanders in the Stanley Cup finals, four games to two.

Chapter 11
CHASING THE CUP

The 1980–81 season marked the zenith in what has become known as the "era of good feelings" in the history of the Minnesota North Stars.

Attendance was up (a 13,094 regular-season average in 1979–80), the Fighting Saints had folded, there was no competition from the WHA and there were no professional basketball teams to siphon off fans. The North Stars had finished third in the Adams Division in the previous season and advanced to the semifinals of the Stanley Cup playoffs before losing to Philadelphia four games to one. The team had a legitimate poster-boy star in Bobby Smith plus up-and-comers Steve Payne, Tommy McCarthy and Craig Hartsburg. Much-anticipated rookie Neal Broten had been brought in for a three-game trial. Goaltending was supplied by the reliable duo of Donny Beaupre and Gilles Meloche. Life was good. "We had an outstanding team that year," recalled general manager Lou Nanne. "We had good team leadership and good camaraderie."

On the management side, the Gopher connection was clicking with University of Minnesota All-American Nanne as GM, his former coach John Mariucci as his assistant and another previous U of M coach, feisty Glen Sonmor, behind the bench. "Sonmor did a magnificent job of coaching and really had the team ready to play," Nanne remembered.

In the regular season, the North Stars had finished 35-28-17, good for third place again in the Adams Division. In December, they started a five-game win streak that saw them knock off Detroit, Winnipeg, Colorado, Philadelphia and Washington. At season's end, Smith led the team in scoring with twenty-nine goals and sixty-four assists, a total of ninety-three points. Next was Tim Young with sixty-six points and Al MacAdam with sixty. Payne had fifty-eight.

The playoffs began for the Stars on April 8, 1981, at the Boston Garden. There, Minnesota defeated the Bruins 5–4, with Payne scoring the game-winning goal. The North Stars went on to sweep the Bruins three games to none. Next came the quarterfinals and the Buffalo Sabers. Payne scored in the first twenty-two seconds of overtime to give Minnesota a 4–3 win in Game One. Game Two was a 5–2 North Star win, and the team took a 3-0 lead in the series at Met Center with a 6–4 win before a crowd announced at 15,784. The following night, the Sabers won 5–4 in overtime but lost the crucial fifth game at home, 4–3, with Minnesota's MacAdam scoring the game-winner.

The semifinals opponent was the Calgary Flames. Only one year before, this team was known as the Atlanta Flames.

These Flames, like Atlanta itself when General Sherman invaded, were doomed from the start. The NHL had granted Atlanta a franchise in 1972, the same year that the outlaw WHA opened for business and was pirating players by offering big money to those who would jump. In retrospect, any time was a bad time for the game of hockey amidst the Georgia peach trees, as the Atlanta Thrashers' organization would later learn.

The Omni Sports Group, headed by Tom Cousins, sold the Flames to Vancouver-based businessman Nelson Skalbina for $16 million, which, at the time, was considered to be an exorbitant sum. Team general manager Cliff Fletcher later recalled that Cousins "turned his whole experience into a profitable one."

In Calgary, the team retained the Flames nickname despite its lack of local relevance, except possibly for oil well fires. Nevertheless, the Flames were wildly popular from the start. Not that many Calgarians could actually see the team play. Home ice was the Stampede Corral, which had only 6,500 seats. The comfy confines of the Corral inspired the Flames to sustain only five losses inside the building during that inaugural season while winning twenty-five and tying ten. "It was a very successful first season," recalled Fletcher. His star player was Kent Nilsson, who accumulated 131 points that season.

Prior to facing the North Stars in the playoffs, Calgary had disposed of Chicago and Philadelphia and, with home-ice advantage, looked to advance to the Stanley Cup finals. It was not to be.

Records show that, somehow, 7,226 fans were squeezed into the Corral for the opener on April 28, 1981. They left disappointed, as the North Stars stunned the Flames with a 4–1 spanking. Two days later, the tables were turned as rookie winger Kevin Lavalle scored the winning goal in a 3–2 Calgary triumph.

The next two contests were held at Met Center before sellout crowds and saw the North Stars winning both contests by the scores of 6–4 and 7–4, sending the entire state into a hockey frenzy. Those who couldn't buy tickets watched the games on television and rushed to newsstands to read about their hockey heroes.

Back at home for Game Five, the Flames refused to go gently into the night, smacking the Stars 3–1 behind right-winger Bob MacMillan. Then it was back to Met Center, where Minnesota won the series four games to two with a 5–3 triumph. Brad Palmer got the game-winning goal.

(In August 1981, local interests bought out Skalbina. One of the new owners was a chap by the name of Norm Green. More on him later.)

By now, North Stars merchandise was flying off the shelves of sporting goods stores from Minneapolis to Albert Lea and from Duluth to Roseau. Everyone, it seems, had to have a North Stars cap or T-shirt (replica jerseys were not commonly sold then).

Brimming with confidence on the heels of the Calgary series, Minnesota on May 12 journeyed to the Nassau County Coliseum in Long Island to face the hated and feared Islanders, defending Stanley Cup champions. When it was over, the Islanders and their famed "Trio Grande" line of Bryan Trottier, Mike Bossy and Clark Gilles retained possession of the Cup.

The wonderment of actually playing for the Stanley Cup stunned the North Stars players, and it showed on the Coliseum ice. The Islanders scored twice while short-handed in the first period, and Minnesota was cooked. It was 4–0 toward the end of the second period when Kent-Erik Andersson scored on a rebound shot past goalie Billy Smith. It was too little, too late. Wayne Merrick answered for New York, and it was 5–1. The final score read: New York 6, Minnesota 3.

"We can't play any worse than we did," fumed GM Louie Nanne after the game. "We didn't test the Islanders. They have a helleva team, and we didn't push them at all. We were tentative and jittery at the outset, and we didn't have good effort."

The effort was better in the second game, but the result was the same. Rookie Dino Ciccarelli scored on a power play three minutes into the game, but seconds later, Mike Bossy answered with a goal of his own to knot the score.

The Bossy goal opened the floodgates for the New Yorkers as Bob Nystrom and Denis Potvin slipped goals past North Star goaltender Don

Free agent right-winger Dino Ciccarelli holds the NHL record for goals by a rookie in a single playoff year (fourteen in 1980). He was inducted into the Hockey Hall of Fame in 2010. *Walt Berry photo.*

Beaupre. The period ended with a 3–1 Islanders' lead. The gritty North Stars got the only score of the second period, a goal by Palmer. Then, only thirty seconds into the third period, Payne scored to tie the game. Minnesota missed a golden opportunity to take the lead with a power play opportunity three minutes later. That seemed to take all the steam out of the Minnesota attack. Potvin scored again, then Ken Morrow, then

Bossy, and it was over. The Islanders had a two-games-to-none advantage heading to Met Center.

"The Islanders special units out-performed us in both games in New York," North Stars defenseman Greg Smith said. "Tuesday [May 12], it was the penalty killers that won it for them. Thursday [May 14], it was the power play."

A sold-out crowd of 15,784 North Stars fanatics watched the hometown team blow leads of 2–0 and 3–1 against the mighty Islanders and fall to defeat. Goals by Steve Christoff and Payne in the first period got Minnesota started. Bossy scored to pull the Isles within one, but Smith answered, and it was 3–1 at the end of the period. "It was by far our best effort," said coach Sonmor, "but it wasn't good enough."

The Islanders came storming back in the second period. Nystrom scored, and then Butch Goring found the net against goalie Meloche to make it 4–3 at the period's end. The Stars regrouped, and a Payne goal knotted the score, but Bossy put New York up 5–4. The pesky Goring then broke through for his third goal, and that was the game-winner.

"We got careless," lamented Sonmor, "and it cost us."

"We were forcing them," said right-winger Kent-Erik Andersson. "We chased them into making mistakes, but after the first period, instead of forcing them, we stopped at the blue line."

In other words, the North Stars began playing not to lose rather than playing to win, and it cost them. Now they were down three games to none in the battle for the Stanley Cup.

To their credit, the team did not fold, as expected, in the fourth game of the series. With the score tied at 2 at the end of the second period, goals by Payne and Bobby Smith gave Minnesota a 4–2 victory. Three of the four goals were scored on power plays. It was to be the team's only win of the series. Perhaps it was overconfidence, or maybe the Islanders wanted to win the Cup at home, but the New Yorkers stopped attacking and played listless hockey in the final period.

Given the energy boost that always seems to infuse champions on home ice, the New York Islanders soared past the North Stars, 5–1, at the Nassau County Coliseum. The first goal came at 5:12 of the first period when a Minnesota clearing pass ricocheted off referee Bryan Lewis and onto the stick of the Islanders' Bob Bourne, who, in turn, fed Goring, who scored off goalie Beaupre. It was that kind of night for the Stars.

New York's line of Wayne Merrick, John Tonelli and Bob Nystrom was again magnificent. Merrick scored the second goal less than a minute after

Goring's tally, and that was all she wrote for the North Stars. As commentator Don Cherry might say, "They were done like dinner."

The Merrick-Tonelli-Nystrom line got their eighteenth goal of the playoffs, all at even strength. Goring scored a pair of goals and was awarded the Conn Smythe Trophy as Most Valuable Player. He had scored ten playoff goals.

Had the North Stars somehow won the Stanley Cup, the Smythe Award would have gone to left-winger Payne, who had scored a remarkable seventeen playoff goals. Payne was philosophical in defeat when he said, "We need a little more experience and consistency to go all the way. And that day will come."

For the North Stars, it never did.

A better prophet was New York's Trottier, who said, "You win [the Cup] once, and you want to win it again and again and again."

And that is precisely what the remarkable New York Islanders did as they won four straight Stanley Cup championships in 1980, 1981, 1982 and 1983, duplicating the feat of the Montreal Canadians in 1976, 1977, 1978 and 1979. Such back-to-back runs will never again be matched.

The Islanders were popular stateside because they were based in the States. Detroit had won five Stanley Cup championships from 1942 to the expansion years but never four in succession.

It's interesting to note that Nassau County, Long Island, might have never had a franchise were it not for the World Hockey Association. Driven to panic by the WHA's New York Raiders franchise, the NHL hastily arranged to establish expansion franchises in Uniondale, New York, and Atlanta. The league had expanded from twelve to fourteen teams only two years earlier and had no plans to expand again for a while, but NHL president Clarence Campbell wanted the new Nassau Veterans Memorial Coliseum for the NHL.

Atlanta was an afterthought since Campbell reasoned that expansion should always occur in pairs. Of course, the league had to be taught not once but twice that Atlanta is not a hockey hotbed.

Campbell eventually was successful in driving the WHA out of New York (the Raiders became the New Jersey Knights and then moved as far away as they could—to San Diego).

Beginning with their third season in the NHL, the Islanders made the playoffs fourteen straight times. Between 1980 and 1984, the Isles won nineteen consecutive playoff series, a streak halted by Wayne Gretzky's Edmonton Oilers, ironically a former WHA franchise.

Not unlike the North Stars, the Islanders franchise was to fall victim to money woes, bad ownership, incompetent management, low attendance and an arena that was aging rapidly.

For decades, Islander management sought assistance from the city, county and state in improving or replacing the crumbling Veterans Memorial Coliseum. None was forthcoming. By 1997, owner John Pickett had had enough. He sold the club for $165 million to a Texan named John Spano. The problem was no one knew who Spano was. No matter. Commissioner Gary Bettman and the NHL welcomed Spano with open arms.

The hitch was that Spano was a con artist, an expert forger. Somehow, he conned the Fleet Bank of Boston into loaning him $80 million, but Spano didn't have the rest of the $165 million. He was supposed to wire a $5 million payment but sent $5,000 instead. Checks he wrote bounced, and he was finally revealed as a complete and utter fraud.

Bettman and the league had failed to do anything that resembled a background check on this charlatan.

Spano eventually was convicted and sentenced to seventy-one months of prison time for bank and wire fraud. Pickett had to take back the Islanders, and the NHL had to absorb another black eye, not its first since the league was founded in 1917.

The Islanders will be leaving their island in 2015, bound for Brooklyn and the Barclays Center. The reason for the delay? The team must honor the lease at the deteriorating Nassau Veterans Memorial Coliseum.

Chapter 12
ENTER GRETZKY

The 1983–84 season would see the Minnesota North Stars finishing first in the NHL's Norris Division, with eighty-eight points based on thirty-nine wins, thirty-one losses and ten ties, and entering the playoffs with high hopes. Little did the North Stars organization realize that it would serve as the facilitator for ending one dynasty, the New York Islanders, and the start of another, the Edmonton Oilers.

The previous season had ended on a sour note. After blitzing through the regular season with a then-record forty wins and defeating the Toronto Maple Leafs three games to one in the playoffs, the Stars went to pieces and were ousted from the tournament by the Chicago Blackhawks in five games.

For the 1983–84 season, Minnesota retained its top goal scorers: Neal Broten, Brian Bellows, Dino Ciccarelli and Brad Maxwell. Goaltending was split between veterans Gilles Meloche and Don Beaupre. Missing was crowd favorite Bobby Smith.

On October 28, 1983, general manager Lou Nanne traded Smith to Montreal for Keith Acton and Mark Napier. "The most difficult one I ever made," Nanne recalled later, "the one trade that still bothers me to this day, was Bobby Smith."

During his years as general manager of the North Stars, Nanne traded more players than any of his contemporaries. In some circles, he was known as "Trader Lou." But the Smith trade was a tough one. According to Nanne, Smith and his agent, Art Kaminsky, requested a trade. At first, Nanne refused. "He wanted to be traded," Nanne said, "because he felt he was not getting enough

NEAL BROTEN
MINNESOTA NORTH STARS

The University of Minnesota connection was clicking when the North Stars got Hobey Baker Memorial Trophy winner Neal Broten (Roseau, Minnesota), who later would have his number retired. *U.S. Hockey Hall of Fame.*

playing time." It was the classic "play me or trade me" scenario. (Records indicate that Smith played in seventy-seven of eighty games in 1982–83, accumulating twenty-four goals and fifty-three assists.)

"I had to trade him," Nanne remembered, "and it really hurt. He was the first player I ever drafted, and he was a real star."

Smith went on to win a Stanley Cup with Montreal. "We also received a second-round pick in the deal," Nanne recalled. (Smith would return to the North Stars in 1990 at the age of thirty-two, but his glory days were past.)

Acton scored seventeen goals with the North Stars and Napier thirteen, but Nanne's best trade of the season involved the return of St. Paul native Paul Holmgren to the Land of 10,000 Lakes. At six-foot-three and 210 pounds, the rugged Holmgren was an authority figure to be reckoned with on the ice.

The 1984 playoffs began in Bloomington with the North Stars facing the same Blackhawks that had knocked them out of the playoffs in both 1982 and 1983. Goalie Murray Bannerman had been highly instrumental in creating North Stars' frustration in both series and was in top form in the opener on April 4, 1984. However, Minnesota led 1–0 on a goal by Lars Lindgren, who had tallied only three goals all season. The lead held up until Chicago's Al Secord, another tormentor to the Stars, scored a pair goals in the third period and Bob Murray got an empty-netter. Final score: Chicago 3, Minnesota 1.

"It was just a question of who capitalized on the breaks," North Stars coach Bill Mahoney said after the game. "There's no question that with a little bit of luck, we could have converted on more of the good chances."

Mahoney was known as a demanding, no-nonsense taskmaster who read and saved clippings of everything newspaper people wrote about him. Consequently, he held grudges.

The second game of the series turned into all-out warfare. The North Stars grabbed a 2–0 first-period lead on goals by Gordie Roberts and Curt Giles, only to see that lead evaporate after goals by Jeff and Steve Larmer and Rick Patterson. A Keith Acton goal tied it at 3, and Al MacAdams's goal put Minnesota ahead to stay. Willi Plett and Neal Broten added goals, and the North Stars hung on for a 6–5 win. "Right from the start," said Steve Payne, "it was a checking, grinding game." Minnesota, the NHL's most penalized team during the regular season, had out-muscled the Blackhawks at home, and now the series shifted to Chicago.

"Other teams have goons; we have equalizers," Nanne said. The "equalizers" he referred to were Plett, Holmgren and Brad Maxwell. Defenseman Maxwell was known for, during the course of a NHL game, standing up after warming the bench and cold-cocking an opponent as he skated past, a maneuver straight out of the movie *Slap Shot*. But Maxwell was more than a thug. In the 1983–84 regular season, he scored nineteen goals and contributed fifty-four assists.

The North Stars won the third game of the series, but the *Minneapolis Tribune* the following day chose to lead the sports section with a lengthy account of a no-hitter pitched the night before by Jack Morris. And this was before Morris became a member of the Minnesota Twins. Hockey has its place, but now this is baseball season in the Upper Midwest.

The North Stars were determined to beat the Blackhawks on foreign ice. Three fights were started before the game was two minutes old. Then Lindgren slipped a goal past Bannerman in the first period, followed by a goal by Acton, and that was all Minnesota needed. "A considerable weight has been lifted from our shoulders," Mahoney proclaimed. The euphoria didn't last. The next night, Chicago evened the series at two games apiece with a 4–3 win. The Blackhawks rallied for two goals in the final eight minutes of the game, with Troy Murray scoring the game-winner on a breakaway.

The fourth game of the series was as violent as the others. In particular was the slashing penalty handed out to Secord. Mahoney was adamant: "Secord took a two-handed swing with his stick. That was a deliberate attempt to injure. That should have been a match penalty." It wasn't. Hey, this is Chicago.

The year before and the year before that, Chicago had knocked the North Stars out of the Stanley Cup playoffs. Now they were about to do it again, but Minnesota held home ice. A crowd of 15,603 jammed into Met Center to watch the event and went away happy. The jinx was broken.

Minnesota held a 41–21 shots-on-goal advantage and beat Bannerman and his Black Hawks 4–1. Bearded Dennis Maruk scored a pair of goals (the second was an empty-netter), and George Ferguson was credited with the game-winner. The monkey was off the North Stars' backs.

"We worked for it," said Payne, "and we took it."

The next opponent was Expansion Six rival St. Louis Blues, who were meeting Minnesota in the playoffs for the first time since 1972, when the Blues knocked the North Stars out of the quarterfinals. The Stars had home ice advantage and benefited from it in a sloppy, penalty-filled contest. St. Louis took a 1–0 lead in the second period on a goal by Pat Hickey, but Ciccarelli won it for Minnesota in the third.

"St. Louis," said defenseman Curt Giles, "plays a very tight-checking game. Whoever makes the least mistakes wins." The free-styling Ciccarelli added that coach Mahoney "wants us to play a defensive-style game. That's okay. I can go both ways."

Expectations of taking a 2-0 lead on home ice were dashed when St. Louis's Doug Gilmore scored a backhanded goal at 16:16 of overtime to defeat the North Stars 4–3. A Plett goal had given Minnesota a 3–1 second-period lead, one the team could not hold.

At home, the Blues took a 2-1 series lead, defeating the Stars 3–1, with Doug Wickenheiser getting the game-winner for St. Louis. The North Stars came out flat and were "outhit, out-checked, and out-hustled," according to Dennis Brackin of the *Minneapolis Tribune*. "They established forechecking before we did," explained Holmgren.

Minnesota rebounded on April 16 on the strength of goals by Bellows and McCarthy, previously held in check by the Blues. Goalie Beaupre turned back thirty-three shots, including twelve in the third period, in a 3–1 North Stars win. It was back to Minnesota for Game Five. Now it was the Blues' turn to play lethargic hockey. The North Stars blitzed St. Louis with goals by Payne, Craig Levie, Acton, Maruk, Plett and Broten for a 6–0 win. It was twenty-two-year-old goalie Beaupre's first career NHL shutout.

Facing elimination, the Blues rallied at home to tie the series at three. Game Seven, however, would be played at Met Center before 15,603 screeching hockey nuts. The crowd was collectively near hoarse by the time Payne scored the unassisted game-winning goal six minutes into overtime in what some believe to be the greatest hockey game ever played at Met Center. Mark Reeds's third-period goal had given St. Louis a 3–2 lead, but Plett tied the game at the 14:21 mark. Payne, who received the nickname "Mister April" for his playoff heroics, consistently maintained that all NHL players are lacking in intensity during the regular season but kick it into a higher gear, diving to stop pucks, in playoff action.

Now in the NHL semifinals, the North Stars needed to get past Edmonton to get to the Stanley Cup finals. Little did they know that the Oilers were sitting on the cusp of greatness. No former World Hockey Association team had ever won the Stanley Cup, but one organization was destined to do so in 1984, and the North Stars would be merely a blip on the radar for the hard-charging Oilers.

Edmonton had in its arsenal a weapon that no team ever had before or since: Wayne Gretzky, the greatest hockey player ever to strap on a pair of skates. Gretzky had been playing in the WHA since he was seventeen because that league welcomed teenagers. Now, against the North Stars in that first playoff game, he was twenty-two. Gretzky scored on a slap shot from the left face-off circle for a 2–0 Oiler lead. Then, in the second period, he corralled the puck at his own blue line, carried it over the Minnesota blue line and deftly slipped it to Jari Kurri, who scored from the right face-off circle. That made it 4–0. The final was Edmonton 7, Minnesota 1, and the North Stars were cooked.

Gretzky was so good that the temptation was always there for opponents to stand back and watch him perform, whether he possessed the puck or not. By the time his career was over, he held an amazing forty regular-season records, fifteen playoff records and six all-star game records. Gretzky finished with 894 NHL goals and 1,963 assists. In fact, if he had never scored a single goal, his assist total alone would make him the all-time scoring leader. His uniform number (99) has been retired league-wide.

Unable to stop Gretzky, the North Stars opted to take out goalie Grant Fuhr in Game Two. Three minutes into the third period, with the score tied 3–3, Holmgren crashed into Fuhr, injuring the goalie's left elbow and sending him to the bench. Andy Moog replaced Fuhr and outplayed his predecessor, making six saves and blanking Minnesota for the balance of the game.

Edmonton had jumped to a 2–0 first-period lead, and it appeared another route was in store, but Broten scored, and then Payne passed the puck between his legs to Plett, who nailed a twelve-footer. The score was tied 2–2. Gretzky then set up Kurri, who scored from the left face-off circle. Minnesota came back with a Brian Bellows breakaway goal. With the score knotted at 3, who else but Gretzky would decide the outcome? On the power play, Gretzky attacked the crease and scored on his own rebound at 6:01 of the third period. The Oilers led the series two games to none heading to Met Center.

Those fans who don't fancy close-checking, 2–1 hockey games were rewarded with thirteen goals on April 28, 1984. Unfortunately for the majority of the 15,784 spectators on hand, eight of those goals were scored by the Edmonton Oilers.

After falling behind 2–0 on goals by Gretzky and Dave Lumley, the North Stars summoned up all their strength and scored an amazing five second-period goals in succession. The scoring parade featured a pair of goals each from Broten and Napier. This only served to make the Oilers annoyed. Gretzky and company quickly retaliated with six goals in a row past a discombobulated Beaupre.

Down 7–5, the North Stars tried a new way (for them) to stop Gretzky in the third period. They tackled him. Gretzky was awarded a penalty shot after being dragged to the ice from behind by Gordie Roberts. A Gretzky backhand penalty shot past the weary Beaupre made it 8–5.

To the North Stars' credit, they did show up at Met Center for Game Four and actually put forth the effort to make it a good game. After a scoreless first period, Don Jackson of Edmonton scored on a two-on-two break at 4:58. The Oilers held that 1–0 lead into the final period, when Ken Linseman scored on a power play. Ciccarelli's forty-footer closed the gap to 2–1, but it was too late. Kurri scored on an empty-netter with forty seconds left, and it was 3–1. Game, set, match. "I thought we had a sensational effort," said coach Mahoney after the game, "one of the finest hockey games we played all year. It was an intense battle every shift. It was a delight to be involved in it." Assistant coach Murray Oliver added, "It could have been a blowout, but we gave them all they could handle."

As for the Oilers, they would go on to win the Stanley Cup finals, dethroning the four-time champion New York Islanders four games to none and starting a dynasty all their own.

Chapter 13

CRAZY

So what went wrong?

Sports historians point to a number of factors leading to the demise of the Minnesota North Stars in 1993. Certainly, the death of the team was not part of a five-year plan announced by the North Stars on April 23, 1987.

That plan envisioned a golden future headed by general manager Lou Nanne, director of player development Glen Sonmor and a new coach, the peerless leader, Herb Brooks, father of the 1980 "Miracle on Ice" at Lake Placid, New York. This was to be the supreme melding of the greatest hockey minds in Minnesota. The possibilities seemed endless.

"I believe in players," Brooks said at the time, "and I believe they want to achieve the ultimate—that they want to take advantage of their God-given talents."

He was wrong. His players failed to use what the Lord had bestowed upon them.

Herb Brooks was a man with few failures on his résumé. This was a big one.

Brooks coached for one season with the North Stars (1987–88). Prior to that, he had successfully coached the New York Rangers from 1981 to 1985. In Minnesota, he had won three NCAA championships with the Golden Gophers. But his record with the North Stars was only 19-48-13 for fifth place in the five-team Norris Division. Obviously, the North Stars did not make the playoffs.

Nanne blamed player injuries for the miserable season, but future Hall of Famer Dino Ciccarelli and Brian Bellows were around long enough to register eighty-six and eighty-one points, respectively. However, injuries to Broten and Payne diluted both players' effectiveness.

"Every time we talked," wrote John Gilbert in his book *Herb Brooks*, "Herbie said that key injuries forced him to back off on his free-flowing system in favor of a more conservative, pragmatic approach" to the game of hockey.

It was revealed that Nanne had earlier tried to hire Brooks before he had settled on Bill Mahoney, but Herb's agent, Art Kaminsky, insisted on a severance package were he to be dismissed. Nanne refused. Another time, Nanne offered Brooks the job, but the pair could not agree on terms for contract length.

But now that Nanne had finally snared Brooks as his head coach, it was driving him crazy.

In his autobiography, *A Passion to Win*, Nanne candidly reveals his battle with obsessive compulsive disorder (OCD): "From as far back as I can remember, I would always do things to extremes. Even as a youngster I was very set in my ways—especially before a game. I would eat the same food at the same time at the same place. As I got older, my obsessions got worse as the intensity increased. By the time I was general manager of the North Stars, my obsessive compulsive disorder was out of control."

The problem was that Nanne didn't realize he had OCD. Then he was asked to be a guest on *The Oprah Winfrey Show*. Prior to the taping, he met with other sports personalities there to appear with him on what he thought was to be a discussion of various superstitions held by each. He soon realized they were talking about OCD. "It hit me like a thunderbolt," Nanne recalled. "What I have is obsessive compulsive disorder, not just a bunch of superstitions." Oprah Winfrey had performed another of her many miracles.

Losing games had been eating Nanne up, and losing was common for the 1988 North Stars. "I was trying everything to win," he remembered. "If we won one night, then the next game I would do everything that I had done for the previous game in hope of winning again. I would take the same route to work, listen to the same radio station, drive in the same lane, eat the same meal at the same time…"

It got so bad that, at mealtime, he found himself trying to hold a fork the same way he had the night the team won. If the North Stars lost, he would fall into a deep depression, speaking to no one.

Finally, a psychiatrist was consulted, and Nanne got what all OCD patients receive: a prescription for antidepressants. The pills worked for a while, but then the guilt common to those born in the 1940s to working-class parents took over. "What am I doing?" Nanne wondered. "I have to take pills to do my job. This isn't right. Nothing good can come from it."

So it was back to the old OCD symptoms. Nanne would have to dress a special way, grasp a phone in a certain manner and systemize his stroll through the press box. "I would walk around a chair four times one way and then four more times another way," he said.

What others might have thought was an amusing foible was becoming a serious disorder. Nanne was losing weight and feeling nauseous. He looked like hell.

Nanne went to the Gund brothers and told them he had had enough. They sent Lou and his wife, Francine, on vacation. The couple returned, but Nanne's mind was made up. He was quitting. The Gunds allowed him to stay as team president.

"Unfortunately," Nanne recalled, "while I was on vacation, Herbie [Brooks] went to the Gunds and said, 'I want a five-year contract as general manager and coach, or I'm quitting at the end of the year.'"

The Gunds did not respond well to intimidation. They told Brooks to put his beautiful Olympic laurels where the sun doesn't shine. They had hired Jack Ferreira as general manager. Ferreira, in turn, named Pierre Page as head coach.

Another version of the Brooks story is told by his biographer, Gilbert, who maintained that Herb was perfectly willing to stay as coach under Ferreria. Brooks told Gilbert that meetings with Ferreria were "cordial," and Herb was invited to continue as coach.

It is here that the two stories converge. Both reach the same conclusion. The Gund boys wanted Brooks out. Case closed. Nanne's grand five-year plan lasted less than a year.

Looking back at the Nanne years prior to his hiring of Brooks, hockey fans note that since 1978, five different coaches—Harry Howell, Glen Sonmor, Murray Oliver, Bill Mahoney and Lorne Henning—had eventually failed to please Nanne.

Nanne's ten-year reign as general manager was also marked by maneuvers that brought high draft choices to the team, including Bellows, the most sought-after junior player since Wayne Gretzky. In 1979–80, the twenty-five-year-old Bellows scored fifty-five goals and chalked up forty-four assists for ninety-nine points but never reached the latter number again. He was traded to Montreal in 1992.

But with the number-one pick in the 1983 draft, Nanne surprised the hockey world by selecting Brian Lawton of New Brunswick, New Jersey, leaving on the board future Hall of Famers Steve Yzerman and Pat LaFontaine. Lawton, an otherwise decent player, never scored more than

In the 1983 draft, general manager Lou Nanne ignored future Hall of Famers Steve Yzerman and Pat LaFontaine to select Brian Lawton of New Brunswick, New Jersey. *Walt Berry photo.*

forty-four points in five years in Minnesota.

All professional sports teams from football to soccer build through the draft. Nanne's record on draft day was less than stellar. By 1990, only six of the players he drafted between 1980 and 1985 were still in the NHL. He blamed his talent scouts for feeding him misinformation.

"As the general manager of a professional hockey team," Nanne wrote, "the pressure is tremendous day in and day out. Mistakes are something you must avoid. You had to make sure you drafted the right players, make sure you made the right trades, signed the right kind of contracts, and above all in the process, win! You had to win. It was the ultimate goal. And when you did win, it was the highest of highs, and when you lost, it was the lowest of lows."

With the North Stars, it was too frequently the latter.

Of his six coaches (including Brooks), only Sonmor (174-161-82) and Mahoney (42-39-12) left with winning records.

The Gund brothers, meanwhile, were plotting to divest themselves of their Minnesota investment. Season ticket sales had dropped from a high of six thousand when the popular Brooks was hired. The following season, the number of season tickets sold dipped below four thousand. The Gunds had seen this happen in Cleveland and were not about to go through it again.

The 1988–89 North Stars, under general manager Ferreria and coach Page, finished third in the Norris Division with the unspectacular record of 27-37-16 and were quickly eliminated from the playoffs by St. Louis, four games to one. Only 8,013 showed up for the last home game of the series, a 5–4 win.

The Gunds' father, George the elder, had been worth $600 million at the time of his demise, and his boys profited from their inheritance, living comfortably—George in San Francisco and Gordon in Princeton, New Jersey.

Absentee ownership of Minnesota teams is a problem that rears up from time to time, owing to the paucity of billionaire sportsmen residing in the state. The state's tax codes aren't openly inviting to the mega-rich. Hence, Minnesota's current NFL and NHL teams are owned by residents of New Jersey and Wisconsin, respectively.

Neither George nor Gordon Gund had any sentimental ties to the Upper Midwest, and on January 30, 1990, with the North Stars' record at 24-26-3, they announced that unless the Metropolitan Sports Commission coughed up $15 million to remodel Met Center, the team would move to an unspecified location. Oh, and fans needed to buy six thousand season tickets within three weeks.

The commission and the City of Bloomington said no to hockey, and the hunt was on for a local buyer to step forward and relieve the Gunds of their North Star burden. There were no serious volunteers.

It was during this period that the NHL board of governors was considering another of the league's forays into expansion. Since the Expansion Six, the NHL had expanded to include the Vancouver Canucks, Buffalo Sabers, Washington Caps, New Jersey Devils, Calgary Flames and New York Islanders, plus four former WHA teams.

Howard Baldwin, former part owner of the Hartford Whalers, and Morris Belzberg, chief executive of Budget Rent-a-Car, were seen nosing around the Bay Area, scouting for a possible franchise location, and this annoyed George Gund. He thought the Bay Area was his exclusive region. If anyone was going to get a franchise there, it would be him (and his brother, of course).

Out of this evolved one of the most atrocious schemes in professional sports history, one that planted the seeds of the destruction of the North Stars.

Chapter 14

DECONSTRUCTION

The NBA returned to Minnesota in 1989 in the form of the Timberwolves, and the timing could not have been worse for the Minnesota North Stars.

Then headed by commissioner David Stern, the NBA was and is a marvel of marketing wizardry. People who had never before gone to a basketball game were drawn to the sport that features names like Michael Jordan, Magic Johnson, Larry Bird and Minnesota's own Kevin McHale.

In their first season of operation, the Timberwolves drew 1 million fans to their temporary home in the Hubert H. Humphrey Metrodome in downtown Minneapolis. A home game with the Denver Nuggets drew 49,551.

The Timberwolves were hot. The North Stars were not.

A new $65 million arena was under construction in downtown Minneapolis. The owners of the Timberwolves, Marvin Wolfenson and Harvey Ratner, were constructing, of all things, a hockey arena. This cool new edifice would have a moveable floor. Floor goes up, floor goes down—up for a regulation hockey rink, and down for an NBA basketball court. Back in the day, this was state-of-the-art stuff.

The elaborate arena was constructed as what is known as a design/build project, and with change orders piling up, it soon became a financial burden for Wolfenson and Ratner. With their initial financing having fallen through, the partners were forced to borrow at high interest rates to complete the construction work, which eventually totaled $94 million.

What is interesting is that they needn't have bothered. Wolfenson later testified that the NBA, as a condition of obtaining a league franchise, required the Timberwolves to build a new building in which to house it.

Not so, according to Russ Granik, then the NBA's executive vice-president. "There was no mandate," Granik said.

Wolfenson later said the Timberwolves had five options: (1) the Metrodome, (2) the Minneapolis Auditorium, (3) St. Paul Civic Center, (4) Met Center and (5) a new building. With so many choices, it would seem that it would be easy to choose.

The Minneapolis Auditorium was ruled out immediately. Various remodeling projects had reduced the building's seating capacity to a fraction of what it was when the Minneapolis Lakers called the place home.

The Metrodome, it was decided, was fine for the inaugural season but, looking to the future, would be impractical when the team got better and made the playoffs. Too many conflicts with the Twins loomed.

Wolfenson and Ratner were turned down by St. Paul Civic Center managing director Marlene Anderson, who said she already had too many bookings in March and April to accommodate the NBA during those months when the facility hosted a myriad of tournaments including the popular Minnesota State High School Hockey League Tournament. The Civic Center, she maintained, was a financial success without a professional sports franchise.

The partners next went to the Gund boys. The brothers had first choice on Met Center weekend dates and were known as, to put it mildly, tough negotiators. The boys already had gotten wind that the Civic Center had turned down Wolfenson and Ratner. They had the pair over a barrel.

The Gunds "had us in a position where they could drive a hard deal," Wolfenson said, "so we decided to build our own place."

And it cost them dearly.

George and Gordon Gund had sunk $3.5 million into building twenty suites in Met Center, a necessary move when the sports economics of the day were taken into consideration. But the building needed more—wider concourses, a larger ticket office, upgraded seating and, of course, more suites.

The brothers also eyed the property across the street that once had housed Metropolitan Stadium, erstwhile home of the Vikings and Twins. They put in a bid for the property that included remodeling Met Center. The Metropolitan Sports Facilities Commission turned them down.

The Met Stadium site was eventually sold to some other brothers, the Ghermezians, who built the largest shopping mall in the United States, the ever-expanding Mall of America.

The Gunds were fed up with Minnesota and wanted out. The Bay Area beckoned. Howard Baldwin and Morris Belzberg had discovered that the city of San Jose, fifty miles south of Fisherman's Wharf, was booming and itching for major-league sports. Further, the city, located in the heart of Silicon Valley, was willing to build an arena to house major-league basketball or hockey, preferably hockey.

San Francisco had a spotted past when it came to hockey. Numerous teams had failed between 1928 and 1967. Then came the biggest failure of all, the ill-fated Golden Seals, whose demise after nine years of operation was fathered by George Gund.

Since the Seals went away, the Bay Area had grown to become home to more than 8 million residents, fueled by Silicon Valley and its computer geniuses. San Francisco and its environs was now the nation's fourth media market.

Baldwin and Belzberg might have discovered the San Jose market, but the Gund brothers wanted it. After all, one of them already lived there. What followed is a scheme that surpassed the one the Gunds cooked up when they merged the North Stars and the Barons. They proposed to deconstruct what they had constructed.

The simple way would have been to relocate the Minnesota franchise to San Jose. That was a clean solution. It was quick. Poof, no more North Stars.

Not so fast. There were those on the NHL board of governors, chiefly Bill Wirtz, who eyed the Gunds with suspicion. How could you screw up a team in the heartland of U.S. hockey, where sixteen thousand people routinely show up for a high school game?

The Gunds came up with a plan that would get them an expansion franchise for $18 million instead of the at-the-time NHL asking price of $50 million. Old man Gund didn't make $600 million by being stupid, and his boys were just as clever.

The NHL had previously announced it would not expand until 1992, when the new San Jose arena would open. But Baldwin and Belzeberg wanted an NHL franchise now. So the Gunds sold them one at the discounted price of $32 million. No matter that it was in frigid Minnesota, not sunny California. But by purchasing the North Stars, Baldwin and Belzeberg saved $18 million off the $50 million price for a San Jose expansion franchise.

The Gunds got San Jose.

There's more. The Gunds, who had merged two teams when they entered the league, were now granted the privilege by the NHL of reversing the process. They say you can't unscramble an egg. The Gunds did.

While the league watched, the North Stars would be systematically gutted. We're through the looking glass here, people.

To aid in the transition, the Gund brothers were allowed to take with them to San Jose the rights to their choice of the North Stars' farm system. A lovely parting gift.

For their new team, George and Gordon got twenty-four youths who previously thought they were someday heading for a career in the Twin Cities. The Baldwin/Belzberg North Stars at the end of the 1990–91 season were allowed to protect from the Gunds only fourteen skaters and two goalies. Each of these hockey players must have had at least fifty NHL games under their belt, or they didn't count. This was in addition to an NHL expansion draft by San Jose of all existing teams.

The Gunds, to say the least, were smooth operators. They played the NHL like a fiddle.

"It's a complex transaction," said Robert Caporale, Baldwin's attorney. "It's an agreement that has been designed to create a win-win situation for the Bay Area and the North Stars."

Minneapolis Star Tribune columnist Patrick Reusse saw it another way. "The only thing worse," he wrote, "for Minnesota than losing a hockey franchise is keeping one under the conditions of the agreement." He compared the NHL to "the World Wrestling Federation." Fellow sports columnist Dan Barreio labeled the NHL "an archaic confederation known for fisticuffs and buffoonery."

"That was a great deal for the Gunds, getting that [Bay Area] market for $18 million plus all the North Stars' top players and prospects," Nanne later recalled

When it came time to choose a name for the team, the Gunds appropriately selected the Sharks.

While the Sharks were feasting inland, a serpent was slithering into the garden.

Howard Baldwin and Morris Belzberg now owned a hockey team with no future in a building they did not like.

Nanne was still team president, and he was sent to negotiate with Minnesota Timberwolves owners Marv Wolfenson and Harvey Ratner about obtaining a working arrangement in their new nineteen-thousand-seat downtown Minneapolis building, which was now known as the Target Center. This was right and proper in that Target Center was a hockey building first (floor goes up) and a basketball arena second (floor goes down).

In a world where logic prevails, the North Stars and Timberwolves share the Target Center, Met Center becomes a parking lot for the Mall of America and Minnesota doesn't go seven years without an NHL team.

But no, professional hockey operates in bizarre-o world apart from logic and the natural order of things. Nanne failed his assignment. He and Tony Tavaras, an advisor from Philadelphia, met with the Timberwolves' Wolfenson, Ratner and Bob Stein, former All-American footballer at the University of Minnesota and, at the time, Wolfenson's son-in-law. Everything was going fine until the subject of dasher board advertising came up. (These are the paid ads plastered on the boards near the ice, parts of which are nearly always visible to television viewers.) Nanne, representing his employer, thought the North Stars should get the ad revenue collected for use of the board space. The Timberwolves trio agreed but thought they should get to select the advertisers from a list of team sponsors.

"I have to have the right to sell to my advertisers," Nanne said, pointing out that Target Center was a "Pepsi building" and Met Center a "Coke building." Ratner and Stein said okay. But Wolfenson wouldn't back down. Negotiations collapsed, never to resume.

By now, Baldwin and Belzberg realized that even at a bargain-basement price, they couldn't afford to own a hockey team. Enter the serpent.

Norm Green was a Canadian investor in a telecommunications firm and owner of an unspecified group of companies investing in shopping centers. He was also a self-styled hockey nut who held a minority share of the Calgary Flames during their Stanley Cup run of 1989. Unsatisfied with that, Green wanted a team of his own.

Green loved hockey, and he hated Baldwin and Belzberg. He bought both out and assumed control of the North Stars. What he got was a once-proud franchise on the verge of ruin. A look at the books told him the team's average attendance was 11,354. A closer look showed Green that the number was inflated by some 3,000 freebies and give-away ticket promotions.

No more free tickets was the Green philosophy. The result was that only 5,730 spectators showed up on opening night. But they all paid full price for their seats! The next home game, against the once-mighty New York Islanders, drew just 5,280 (the average per-game attendance in the NHL at this time was 15,000). Players could hear the echoes of spectators conversing with one another other and coughing in the stands.

Then something wonderful happened. The North Stars started to win.

Chapter 15
FLUKE

The North Stars finished the 1990–91 regular season in fourth place in the Norris Division with twenty-seven wins, thirty-nine losses and fourteen ties. A four-game win streak in March boosted attendance and helped the team nose out Toronto and gain a playoff berth.

Minnesota shocked Norris Division champion Chicago in the first round of the Stanley Cup finals, winning four of six games. Brian Bellows got the game-winning goal in the decisive sixth game, which attracted 15,274 fans to Met Center. Those who thought that was a stroke of luck were quick to change their minds when Minnesota proceeded to knock off St. Louis in six games and Edmonton in five, despite lacking home-ice advantage in either series.

This set up a Stanley Cup final round against the newest dynasty on the block, the Pittsburgh Penguins. A fellow member of the Expansion Six, the Penguins had endured a spotted history. The team was accorded only a small amount of interest by the citizens of western Pennsylvania in the team's first two years of existence and drew an average of only 6,008 spectators in 1968–69. By 1975, the team was in extreme financial distress, and rumors flew that the team would relocate to Denver or Seattle. A new ownership, which included former North Stars general manager Wren Blair, was able to pay $3.5 million for the club and fend off the creditors.

The team had quality players such as Syl Apps Jr., Vic Hadfield, Jean Pronovost, Ron Schock and Ron Stackhouse and made the playoffs but still lost $1.5 million.

Pittsburgh had shown it could support major-league baseball and football, but hockey enthusiasts remained on the fringe despite the fact that the Penguins qualified for the playoffs for seven of eight seasons from 1975 to 1982. The team switched uniform colors from blue to the traditional black and gold of the Pirates and Steelers, but this did not prevent the Penguins from having the worst record in the NHL in 1983 and 1984. Pittsburgh tanked the latter season, losing ten of its last twelve games, earning the right to draft Mario Lemieux, the brightest prospect in skates, with the first pick. The league's integrity once again was called into play, especially when Penguin's coach Lou Angotti later admitted to the *Pittsburgh Post-Gazette* that he had guided his team in the direction of defeat in order to draft Lemieux.

Just as "the Great One," Wayne Gretsky, had transformed the Edmonton Oilers into champions earlier, "Super Mario" Lemieux saved hockey in Pittsburgh. The transformation of the Penguins into champions, however, would take longer. Pittsburgh failed to make the playoffs for four seasons, but Lemieux was attracting an increasing number of new fans to the Civic Arena (affectionately known as "the Igloo"). Eventually, management saw fit to surround the six-foot-five, 230-pound Mario with quality teammates, such as former Oiler Paul Coffey, Kevin Stevens, Rob Brown, Jaromir Jagr and goaltender Tom Barrasso. By 1991, the Penguins were in the Stanley Cup finals. Just as they had with the Islanders and Oilers, the North Stars were about to facilitate the emergence of another NHL dynasty.

Throughout its improbable playoff run, Minnesota did not enjoy home-ice advantage. The Stanley Cup finals began at the Igloo on May 15, 1991. A capacity crowd of 16,164 was delighted when Ulf Samuelsson lit the light for the first goal of the series and a 1–0 Penguin lead in the opening period.

Neal Broten then scored, unassisted, the first of his two goals that night. Broten was one of only three North Stars players to have been members of the last Minnesota team in the finals. The other two were Bobby Smith and Curt Giles. Smith was winding down his second stint with the Stars. He returned to Minnesota on August 7, 1990, in exchange for a fourth-round draft choice, an indication of how far his value had diminished.

Ulf Dahlen scored to put the North Stars up 2–1 before Lemieux tied the score with a goal of his own. The score was tied again at three before Broten scored again, and the thirty-three-year-old Smith subsequently got the game-winning goal.

Broten had participated in only three regular-season games before the 1981 playoff run. He remembered how difficult it was for him then to keep up with the high-flying Islanders. "Bryan Trottier would have had to break

Minnesota's all-time favorite player, native son Neal Broten, headed for Dallas with the rest of the North Stars. He would later drink from the Stanley Cup as a member of the New Jersey Devils in 1995. *Walt Berry photo.*

his leg," Broten said, "and Mike Bossy break his arm for us to have a chance to beat those New York Islanders." The Penguins, he observed, were not in the same class with the Isles.

Minnesota's 5–4 win prompted *Minneapolis Star Tribune* columnist Patrick Reusse to proclaim, "There's going to be a victory parade [in downtown Minneapolis]."

Not so fast. Two nights later, the Penguins came back to win 4–1, tying the series and putting a hold on plans for Reusse's parade. Goalie Barrasso made thirty-nine stops in the Pittsburgh victory. The teams battled evenly until Lemieux's goal at 15:04 of the second period, giving the Penguins a 3–1 lead, one they never relinquished.

The series moved to Met Center, and the hopes of the local team soared when it was announced that Super Mario would be a noncombatant. Back spasms sidelined Lemieux. Those among the sellout crowd of 15,378 breathed a sigh of relief and saw the hometown heroes blitz the Pens 3–1.

Dave Gagner and Bobby Smith scored goals only thirty-three seconds apart in the second period, and Pittsburgh was cooked. Gaetan Duchesne added the third goal.

By now, it was obvious that the series was attracting a different type of Twin Cities fan. With a shallow season-ticket base, North Stars' playoff ticket sales were dependent on hard-drinking curiosity-seekers and front-runners, some of whom who had never witnessed a pro sporting event more significant than a wrestling card. The polite "Minnesota nice" fans who once frustrated Wren Blair with their silence were few and far between on May 19 and May 21, the dates of the two consecutive Stanley Cup finals games at Met Center.

North Stars management, aware that the people being let in the building on those two nights could easily turn out to be the American equivalent of European soccer hooligans, wisely beefed up security. "It amazes me," head of security Tom Azzone said after the May 19 game, "what 35-year-old guys do when they are drunk. You wouldn't believe what some people do." What they do is soil themselves, vomit and instigate fisticuffs—even with security personnel. Azzone's crews were instructed to discard their usual neckties in favor of clip-ons. This prevented their being garroted by hockey hooligans.

With a two-games-to-one lead, optimism was running high in the Minnesota locker room before the North Stars took to the ice. Then, before they knew it, the team was behind 3–0.

Pittsburgh scored an amazing three goals in three minutes on the state's favorite fair-haired goalie, Jon Casey, born in Grand Rapids, Minnesota. Unfortunately, Casey is now known as the only goaltender in Stanley Cup finals history to let in so many goals so quickly at the start of a game. The goals came off the sticks of Stevens, Ron Francis and, of course, Lemieux, who was back from his one-game rest. Many of the fans were still finishing alcoholic concoctions in the Met Center parking lot when the history-making event occurred.

Minnesota's Gagner provided a ray of hope when he scored late in the period to make it 3–1, but Bryan Trottier, thirty-four years old and nearing the end of a brilliant career, placed another puck behind Casey, and it was 4–1. Trottier, who had been Broten's nemesis in 1981, continued to plague him in 1991. The North Stars crept to within 4–3 on goals by Brian Propp and Mike Modano, but Phil Bourque salted the game away, scoring on Casey to make it 5–3 Penguins.

The crowd, which had been merely rowdy and surly, now turned ugly. Twenty-something thugs and louts accosted mild-mannered strangers in their seats, insisting they were not cheering loud enough. The zoo-like atmosphere carried over to the parking lot, where numerous fights broke out away from the purview of security guards. The entire evening added up to a black eye for Minnesota hockey fans.

The series returned to the Steel City for Game Five of the series. The North Stars were greeted by hand-painted signs prompting them to remember what happened to the Minnesota Vikings in Super Bowl IX. (The Vikings lost to Pittsburgh, 16–6, and never trailed the Steelers.) Perhaps Casey was pausing to read those signs when he let in four goals in the first thirteen minutes and forty-two seconds of the game. Whether he was or not, coach Bob Gainey had seen enough and yanked Casey in favor of Toronto native Brian Hayward, who everyone knew was going to be one of those talented young North Stars destined to become a San Jose Shark as part of the swindle pulled by the nefarious Gund brothers. Hayward allowed two more Penguin goals (by Ron Francis and Troy Loney), but the game, for all intents and purposes, was decided after those first four goals, scored by Lemieux, Stevens and a twenty-three-year-old Mark Recchi, who had two. To the team's credit, the North Stars did come within 5–4 on goals by Broten, Gagner (two) and Dahlen, but it was to be the last gasp of a tired team from the Upper Midwest.

Down three games to two in the battle for Lord Stanley's Cup, Minnesota limped home for Game Six. The indignity of seeing the visiting team drink from the most treasured trophy in sports history could not be avoided. At least when the North Stars lost in the Stanley Cup battle with the Islanders in 1981, it had happened in Long Island. But shame was destined to dog the North Stars from May 25, 1991, to the end of the team's days.

What happened that May 25 has been variously described as a nightmare, a tragedy and a debacle. Pittsburgh won 8–0. End of story. End of season. End of hope. Members of the ragged and rowdy crowd could only stare and gape stupidly. Samuelsson scored the first goal, and it was all that was needed. But just to make sure the coffin was nailed shut, the Penguins scored seven more. Casey was catatonic and, once again, replaced by Hayward.

By losing 8–0, the North Stars managed to accomplish what no team in the final Stanley Cup series game had since 1905. That year, the Dawson City Nuggets of the Yukon Territory traveled an estimated four thousand miles to meet their destiny. The Nuggets' challenge to the Ottawa Silver Seven was accepted, and the team traveled by dog sled, bicycle, rail and on foot to Skagway to board a ship that took them to Seattle. Then it was on to Vancouver and the Canadian Pacific transcontinental railway bound for

Ottawa. The rigors of travel must have taken a toll. Dawson City lost to Ottawa, 23–2.

The North Stars did not lose to Pittsburgh by twenty-one goals, but 8–0 was too much for Norm Green. "I'm disappointed by the final score," the flustered owner told the *Minneapolis Star Tribune*.

Soon the entire state would be disappointed with Norm Green.

Chapter 16
NORM GREEN

Norm Green was a hockey dilettante. He had little appreciation of Minnesota's hockey tradition or the state itself. He was proud of his Canadian heritage and his success with the Calgary Flames.

Chance put him in Minnesota, and it didn't take long for him to become the most vilified man in the history of organized athletic activity in the state.

The chant "Norm sucks!" became an indelible part of the state sports fans lexicon ahead of even "We hate Iowa."

It wasn't that way immediately. In fact, history notes that the new type of North Stars' fan (boozy, belligerent and crude) took to Green and his wife, Kelly (Kelly Green, get it?), as they arrived with a pair of pet dogs for games in a black Rolls Royce. The "let them eat cake" image was there, invisible to those fools waiting for the Met Center gates to swing open and allow them to reach their favorite *bierstube* inside. They toasted Green, and from his perch in the owner's box, he toasted them back. It was a Roman circus. It didn't last.

A shopping center maven, Green saw his neighbor, the new Mall of America (MOA), as a mall of money for him. He floated proposals past the City of Bloomington and the Metropolitan Sports Facilities Commission. Green wanted a skyway connection to the MOA, site of the former Metropolitan Stadium. He would line the skyway with sports-themed shops and bars and even the U.S. Hockey Hall of Fame, which he would relocate from Eveleth. He wanted free land, zero property taxes and below market-rate financing. He would name his venture the "Avenue of the Stars."

Centerman Mike Modano played all eighty-two games with the ill-fated 1992–93 North Stars, scoring thirty-three goals and assisting on sixty others. His Dallas Stars won the 1999 Stanley Cup. *Walt Berry photo.*

Norm had big plans, but nobody was listening.

On the ice, the 1991–92 North Stars magically returned to the form they had established before the Stanley Cup drive the past season, proving that all of that must have been a mere mirage, an illusion, a trick. The North Stars, now led by Mike Modano, once again finished in fourth place in the Norris Division with a 32-46-6 mark. The club closed the regular season by losing 7 of its last 9 games. Modano had thirty-three goals and forty-four assists for seventy-seven points, tops on the team.

There would be no repeating the glorious playoff run of the previous season. Detroit eliminated Minnesota in the first round of the playoffs. Gerard Gallant, not to be confused with Fighting Saint goon Gord Gallant, scored the winning goal past goaltender Jon Casey in the seventh and final game of the series, won by the Red Wings 5–2.

Minnesota sold out only one of the three playoff games at Met Center, and Green saw this as a portent of things to come. For his team to come close to breaking even, it would have to make the Stanley Cup finals every year, and that was not achievable with the current cast of characters.

Green had since changed the team's uniforms and logo. He had dispatched Nanne, by now one of his minions, to locate someone who was up to the task of creating what Green called the club's "crest." Nanne found a chap named Bill Mack, who did the job for a couple season tickets. Green saw what Mack had drawn and told him if he would eliminate the "North" from "North Stars," he could have the tickets. "It should have occurred to me," said Nanne, "that Norm was thinking of moving the team when the logo on the uniforms was redesigned."

Thus, Stars can be Stars anywhere, even in Anaheim. Norm by now seriously wanted to move the Minnesota franchise to Anaheim but was scared off by the financial might of the Disney empire. Disney subsequently got an expansion team, the Mighty Ducks, named after a Disney movie filmed in part at Met Center.

With Anaheim out of the picture, Green searched for another landing spot for his franchise.

"Maybe people in Minnesota should have listened when the Gunds said they were losing money," Green mused. Maybe Green himself should have stayed out of Minnesota. But he didn't. Now he was stuck in what he saw to be a barren wasteland.

The Twin Cities market was small, Met Center didn't have enough suites or club seating and there were too many teams with which to compete (including those representing the University of Minnesota).

Despite having the lowest ticket prices in the NHL, season ticket sales for the ruinous 1992–93 season did not exceed 6,400. Green claimed to have lost $24 million in the Land of Ten Thousand Lakes. It should be noted, however, that the team he paid $32 million for had increased in market value to $42 million, according to *Financial World* magazine.

It was no secret after the season started that Green was going to do what the Gunds did not—move the team.

The 1992–93 North Stars were better than they were in the previous season and won five of the team's first eight games. On December 26,

Minnesota defeated the Winnipeg Jets at home, 5–4, for an 18-12-5 record. The rivalry with the Jets was especially keen since many Winnipeg residents chose to drive the freeways directly to Met Center and back to Manitoba. That rivalry ended when both teams were transferred to cities where ponds never froze. The North Stars were the first of the two teams to go. That month, the NHL governors granted Green the go-ahead to move. But where?

Norm Green didn't spend all of his time at the office studying maps and globes looking for a new home. From time to time, he could be observed wandering through North Star offices laying on what the British call "busy hands" on the help. He would feel a female worker's shoulder to see if she was wearing a brassiere. He would sneak a peck at another's cheek. He kissed and expected to be kissed in return. He made it clear that he wanted receptionists who were blonde, pretty and exceptionally well endowed. Green was every proper young lady's nightmare, and one young lady had had enough.

Kari Dziedzic, the North Stars' executive assistant to Norm Green, filed a lawsuit claiming inappropriate and demeaning behavior by her employer. Other female employees supported Dziedzic.

Norman Green had chosen to sexually harass a member of one of Minneapolis's most important political families. He didn't stand a chance. Further, Kari Dziedzic chose as her attorney the colorful Ron Rosebaum, legal eagle, radio talk show commentator and prominent defender of the downtrodden.

Green's defense? He tried to hide behind the fact he was Canadian and "didn't know the rules." If one bought Green's defense, U.S. females were fair game the minute they crossed the border. Want to spend a weekend in Calgary? Better bring mace and learn karate. (Incidentally, Kari Dziedzic is currently a Minnesota state senator.)

Green was given the option of moving to downtown Minneapolis or downtown St. Paul but said he needed twelve thousand guaranteed season ticket sales before he'd go. A prominent envelope manufacturer said he'd buy one thousand season tickets. Not interested, said Green.

We now know that his mind was made up before the season had started. He was leaving and taking with him the team that had called Minnesota home for a quarter century. Incredibly, Green did not wait for the end of the 1992–93 season to conclude. He wanted out and fast. He was heading south, toward the Lone Star State. Like Sam Houston before him, he was going to Texas, far south of the Canadian border.

The rumor started before Christmas and gained traction in the months of January and February. Meanwhile, on the ice, Green's players had the sixth-best record in the NHL at the all-star break. On March 9, the North Stars defeated the San Jose Sharks, 4–2, for a 32-27-9 record at that point in the season.

Then the hammer came down. The rumors were correct. On March 10, 1992, the fatal announcement came.

"I'm very proud and excited," Green said without a trace of remorse, "to present to Dallas the National Hockey League." Done. The North Stars were leaving Minnesota. As for the "North" portion of the team's nickname, that could stay in a snow bank somewhere. Green didn't need it any more.

But wait—the NHL had a new commissioner, Gary Bettman, a smooth operator fresh from a job with the NBA. Surely, he would do something to stop this travesty. Or not.

"Dallas came about," Bettman said, "because a team in trouble in the market explored its alternatives." This was now Bettman's NHL. "Money," wrote Jonathan Gatehouse in his Bettman book *The Instigator*, "and the attendant happiness of the owners trumped the desires of fans and communities." Bettman looked at the Twin Cities and saw a population of 2.5 million. Then he looked at the Dallas–Fort Worth area and saw 4 million souls in residence there. The needs of the many outweigh the needs of the few.

Besides, Bettman was new on the job. He indicated that there wasn't much he could do.

"The NHL," columnist Tom Powers wrote in the *St. Paul Pioneer Press*, "bears the responsibility for the travesty of justice that just occurred here. What does Bettman do? He came out and said that we should go without NHL hockey for a while, that maybe the people here would appreciate it more down the road...The people here are at the mercy of the gutless, powerless people in charge of the NHL."

Like naughty children, the hockey fans of Minnesota must have their candy taken away until the paternalistic NHL says they can have it back. So there!

But there was still a season to be completed under the tattered banner of the Minnesota North Stars. Like the baseball Milwaukee Braves before they moved to Atlanta, the North Stars were lame ducks. Not mighty ducks, lame ducks.

On March 11, in Saskatoon, Saskatchewan, Minnesota defeated Vancouver 4–3. Perhaps the news of the sale hadn't reached northern

Saskatchewan, but when the team arrived in St. Louis for the next game versus the Blues, reality bit, and the North Stars lost 6–2. Then, they lost again to the Blues at home, 3–1. They lost again and again and again before tying Toronto 3–3. Then more losses. The team went 0-9-1.

"You say none of the outside stuff should detract you, and it shouldn't. But it did have some effect," commented Bobby Smith. "Everyone was talking about it, and if you weren't talking about it, someone was asking you about it. It was the only subject of conversation."

As for Green, he took the players' wives on a "public relations" tour of the "Big D," where they were wined by Dallas and Fort Worth real estate agents. At the end of the tour, the group was given $9,000 worth of cowboy boots, paid for by Dallas businessmen. Norm was always a lady-killer.

Back in Minnesota, their husbands were blowing their playoff chances.

By now, "Norm sucks!" had turned into a cottage industry in the Twin Cities with special anti-Green sweatshirts, buttons and voodoo dolls selling at a brisk place. The theme song to *The Addams Family* TV show was played at Met Center, but instead of snapping their fingers at the appropriate portion of the ditty, fans screamed, "Norm sucks!"

But Norm didn't hear them. He was barricaded in his stately mansion in Palm Springs, California. He did attend one North Star road game in Los Angeles. A fan poured beer on his head. Green stayed at home after that.

An insight into the brain of Norm Green was given by Lou Nanne, who once was dispatched to Detroit by Green in an effort to see what made the Red Wings and Hockeytown, USA, so successful. Nanne came back with a portfolio full of suggestions, which he presented to Green. "These are lousy ideas," Green told Nanne. His mind was made up ahead of time. It was Green's way or the highway.

Green's personal highway led to Dallas.

Dallas's record in the 1993–94 season was 42-29-13, good for third place in the NHL's new Central Division. The Stars swept St. Louis four games to none in the conference quarterfinals but lost four games to one in the conference semis. Not that anyone in Minnesota cared.

Hockey attendance that first season at Reunion Arena, where the primary tenant was the NBA's Dallas Mavericks, averaged 16,119. The season before, at Met Center, North Star attendance averaged 13,910.

Green held on as owner, waiting for the man with the best offer to unload his team. Fortunately for him, it was not Texan John Spano. Green's mark was Tom Hicks, the affable chairman of the board and chief executive officer of Hicks, Muse, Tate & Furst, a Dallas private investment firm. Green sold the team to Hicks for $84 million and got out of the hockey business. Hicks later found himself in a financial bind, and the NHL had to fund the team.

Green, who reportedly owed $39 million to Canadian bankers, got out before the team reached the pinnacle of success in 1999. The Dallas Stars made the Stanley Cup finals against the Buffalo Sabers. The sixth game, with the Stars leading the series three games to two, went into an unbelievable three overtimes before Brett Hull (Bobby's son) scored the winning goal for Dallas. No matter that Hull's foot was clearly in the crease—the referees were tired and wanted to go home.

Thus, the Stanley Cup, a trophy that had eluded the North Stars, now belonged to the south Stars. No one can imagine the bitter taste in the mouths of Minnesota's legion of hockey fanatics.

Chapter 17
THE ABYSS

I t's obvious we never should have left," said NHL commissioner Gary Bettman on October 11, 2000.

If it was so obvious, Mr. Commissioner, why did you allow it to happen?

But then, why does so little that the NHL does make sense? Why did the league wait so long to expand, and why was expansion such a mess? Why were the Gunds allowed to splice two teams and dismantle what was left? Why was the league forced to operate the failed Phoenix Coyotes? Why so many shady owners? Why do we now have sixteen teams in one conference and fourteen in the other? Why is fighting tolerated and even encouraged? Why do road teams wear white? The questions never end.

The NHL is an enigma with a commissioner as its gatekeeper. Some hockey fans have pointed out that a study of facial characteristics reveals Bettman's uncanny resemblance to Bela Lugosi in the actor's signature movie role as Count Dracula. Be afraid. Be very afraid. Even though Minnesota had a professional hockey team at that sport's highest level, the NHL in those days seemed crude and unpolished when compared to the way the NFL and Major League Baseball do business in the Twin Cities. Even when the North Stars advanced to the Stanley Cup finals, there was doubt about the validity of the NHL. In 1981, eight teams had equal or better regular-season records than Minnesota. In 1991, it was fifteen. What was the point of going to games in November and December?

Two entities stepped into the void left by the North Stars' flight. First, there was the new ten-thousand-seat Mariucci Arena on the University of Minnesota campus. The hockey Golden Gophers played before sellout crowds on a two-hundred-foot- by one-hundred-foot Olympic-sized ice sheet. The first game at the glittering Mariucci ice palace was played on October 30, 1993, and gave fans a hockey fix they couldn't get from the North Stars. Collegians play a cleaner, pass-oriented game where finesse trumps brawling.

Then there was the International Hockey League (IHL) and a Minnesota franchise owned by Kevin McLean and Roger Sturgeon. The St. Paul Civic Center, whose management had earlier said it was too big for the NBA, now suddenly embraced minor-league hockey. Dates that previously were unavailable to accommodate the Minnesota Timberwolves were now opened up for something called the Minnesota Moose. Logic such as this was emblematic of the capital city where an independent minor-league baseball team ruled during Minnesota's three months of summer. Meanwhile, Minneapolis had the Minnesota Twins, a somewhat more credible option.

Minor-league hockey proved to be less alluring in Hockeytown, Minnesota, than minor-league baseball (crowds seldom exceeded four thousand), and after three seasons, the Moose were sent packing (in 1996) to Winnipeg to become the Manitoba Moose. (The franchise today exists as the St. John's Icecaps.) Eventually, the entire IHL disintegrated.

The Winnipeg connection was to play another role in the history of professional hockey in Minnesota. The Winnipeg Jets, charter members of the World Hockey Association and one of four teams plucked from the WHA into membership in the NHL, were floundering in 1995. Even with a small payroll ($13 million), the Jets were hemorrhaging money.

It followed that Minnesota interests would purchase the Winnipeg Jets and move the franchise down the interstate freeway system to Minneapolis or even St. Paul. And so it came to pass that a pair of Minneapolitans, Richard Burke and Steven Gluckstern, were prepared to purchase the Jets for $65 million and move the team to the Target Center.

But Count Dracula had other plans. Minnesota had not suffered long enough. Bettman's master plan was to expand the NHL's continental footprint in the United States. As part of the plan, the Hartford Whalers moved to North Carolina, and the Quebec Nordiques became the Colorado Avalanche. Now, Bettman looked at Phoenix and its television audience potential and liked what he saw. No sentimentalist, he had sparse affinity for Canadian cities, and to him, Minnesota might as well be a province of Ontario. Also, Bettman's NHL was not about to share Target Center with the NBA.

Burke, however, felt a Target Center deal was feasible. All he needed was a guaranteed $8 million per year from the city, the state, the Timberwolves, Ogden Entertainment (arena managers) or whomever. When that was not promised him, Burke turned to St. Paul. The deal offered him there was that he could have the Civic Center as his to manage, collecting all revenue from signage, concessions, parking, etc. The Civic Center would be remodeled at public expense to include thirty to forty luxury seats.

Burke was interested, but as *St. Paul Pioneer Press* columnist Tom Powers suspected, the city was being used "as leverage" for a Phoenix deal.

Fellow columnist Charley Walters reported that Minnesota governor Arne Carlson was "prepared to call legislative leaders together to see if they would act early in the session" to fund Civic Center improvements.

All of this was in vain. The reality was that only an extensive remodeling job could have met Commissioner Bettman's standards for an NHL facility. Contractors would have to replace and raise the roof, tear out all of the seats and completely gut the building. It would be like replacing all the parts of an old auto. It's cheaper to purchase a new one.

On December 4, 1995, St. Paul mayor Norm Coleman held a press conference. "The opportunity," he wailed, "the Winnipeg Jets, is not going to happen in this community."

Pioneer Press columnist Bob Sansevere reacted by calling Burke a "corporate toad" who was demanding a "guaranteed profit" from arenas located in either Minneapolis or St. Paul.

On December 12, Burke signed a letter of intent to move the Winnipeg Jets to Phoenix for the 1996–97 season. A group known as BG Hockey Ventures had purchased the team for $68 million. The famously peevish NHL governors, meeting in West Palm Beach, Florida, united around Bettman as if he were the new messiah. They saw the 17,500-seat America West Arena and said, "Phoenix looks good to us, Mr. Commissioner, please proceed."

To this day, Bettman rules the NHL with an iron fist. He has been described as the most powerful commissioner in professional sports.

Bettman dictated terms of the sale of the Jets over to Burke and a new player on the hockey scene, Phoenix sports mogul Jerry Colangelo. Turns out Coangelo was an old buddy of Bettman from the commish's NBA days. He was confident he and Colangelo could force-feed ice hockey to desert rats, an inflexible attitude that persists to this day.

By 1996, Bettman and the now-subservient NHL board of governors were considering expansion to thirty teams. The owners were in need of a quick

Darby Hendrickson of Richfield, Minnesota, and the University of Minnesota scored the first-ever regular-season goal for the new Minnesota Wild on October 11, 2000. *Walt Berry photo.*

cash flow that expansion teams would ante up.

Applicants were to supply the NHL with $100,000 deposits, an effort to scare away the lunatic fringe. Eleven groups representing nine cities coughed up their deposits. The groups represented: Cleveland, Oklahoma City, Portland, Houston, Orlando, Las Vegas, Nashville, Atlanta and the Twin Cities of Minneapolis and St. Paul.

Bettman and a select group of NHL owners toured the cities (and others), ran background checks on prospective owners and inspected available arenas. In Minnesota, neither Target Center nor the St. Paul Civic Center could pass muster, but he already knew that from the experience with Burke.

Bettman had three rigid criteria. Cities wishing admittance to the NHL must have (1) strong ownership, (2) a proven hockey market and (3) an arena that meets NHL standards. By now, it was apparent that club seating was a cash cow and the key to owner happiness and wealth in hockey. Existing Twin Cities' venues were found lacking. Club seating is a ploy used to make ticket-buyers think they have purchased luxury box seats. For luxury box prices, they get a seat in the arena plus a dining area shared with others, usually strangers. But the public loves it because it gives individuals a sense of entitlement.

Bettman wanted an expansion franchise in Minnesota. He knew of the pent-up frustration and embarrassment the state endured. It was equal to the angst of Cleveland when the NFL's Browns went away. He needed a potential owner, and he found one in Robert O. Naegele Jr., chairman of the board of directors of Naegele Communications Inc.

On June 25, 1997, Bettman announced that Minnesota Hockey Ventures Group LLC, chaired by Naegele, had been awarded an NHL franchise to begin play in the 2000–01 season. The price? $80 million.

According to Brian Murphy of the *St. Paul Pioneer Press*, Naegele had "assembled a group of 13 investors free of financial skeletons and helped secure the civic and community backing to construct a $160-million [arena] that should provide the economic viability that the predecessor building lacked."

The "predecessor building" was the St. Paul Civic Center, and it had to go, and so it did. In its footprint rose what we now know as the Xcel Energy Center. Minnesota legislators supplied $65 million to go toward arena construction. The city and the team's ownership provided the rest.

Of the four expansion franchises granted by Bettman, only Minnesota thrives. Columbus, midway between Cleveland and Cincinnati and chosen to give the NHL an Ohio presence, remains a college town, and the hockey team plays second fiddle to all things Ohio State. Interest in the Nashville Predators runs hot and cold—mainly cold. And Atlanta was a full-blown failure.

Still, in the world of the NHL, one out of four isn't bad.

Chapter 18
INTO THE WILD

On April 10, 1998, the Minnesota state legislature agreed to fund $65 million of the cost of replacing the St. Paul Civic Center. Later, the legislature would meet the needs of the Minnesota Twins, the University of Minnesota football team and the Minnesota Vikings with new stadiums. The hockey team had opened the financing floodgates.

On June 23, a groundbreaking ceremony was held adjacent to the obsolete St. Paul Civic Center. During the ceremonies, demolition work on the twenty-six-year-old Civic Center was underway. Pouring of the foundation of the new building, later known as the Xcel Energy Center, began in October.

Earlier, a crowd of 18,294, the largest such gathering in Minnesota pro hockey history, gathered at Target Center in Minneapolis for an exhibition game between the Dallas Stars and the Phoenix Coyotes. The game pitted the team that Minnesota lost against the team Minnesota should have had. The commissioner could only smile.

The following year, Phoenix was paired with the New York Rangers in an exhibition game at Target Center. This one raised $27,500 for Minnesota youth hockey programs. Remember, Gary Bettman had earlier pronounced Target Center unfit for the NHL.

The new team was to be known as the Wild, an apt nickname because followers of the NHL in the state had been cast out and forced by Bettman to figuratively wander the wilderness, half crazed, until they finally were welcomed back inside the campfire circle of friends. In the process, they became feral. Other (perhaps better) nicknames suggested were Minnesota

The hero of the improbable 2003 playoff run was Andrew Brunette. Note the Wild logo on his chest. What is it? A wolf, a gopher, a lynx? Fans are invited to guess. *Walt Berry photo.*

Blizzard, Minnesota Freeze, Minnesota Northern Lights, Minnesota Blue Ox and Minnesota Voyageurs.

Front office moves drew headlines. First there was genial Jac Sperling, fast on his feet and always ready with a quip. An early hire, the slick Sperling was named chief executive officer. An attorney, Sperling had worked against Minnesota hockey interests when he represented the ownership group that acquired the Winnipeg Jets and relocated that franchise to the Valley of the Sun. But now he was on our side, working for the greater good of Minnesota hockey.

Then there was affable Doug Risebrough, the "Riser," a Canadian through and through. On September 2, 1999, the Riser was appointed executive vice-president and general manager in charge of overall hockey operations, including all matters related to player personnel, coaching staff, scouting and minor-league personnel. Risebrough had been vice-president of hockey operations for the Edmonton Oilers. He also had served as general manager of the Calgary Flames.

The following June, Jacques Lemaire was named the first Wild head coach. A Stanley Cup winner as coach of the New Jersey Devils in 1995, the pugnacious Lemaire and Risebrough spent their playing days in the proud Montreal Canadiens organization. Together, they were instrumental members of Montreal's four consecutive Stanley Cup championships in 1976, 1977, 1978 and 1979. They were hockey royalty.

Perhaps the smartest front-office hire the team made was to pluck St. Paul native Bill Robertson away from the Anaheim Mighty Ducks. As vice-president of communications and broadcasting, "Billy Rob" smoothed the way for the new team with fans, the business community and the media. In working with the latter, he has earned the reputation as the best there ever was and the best there will ever be.

As the NHL faced yet another expansion, it was apparent that sons of Canada alone were unable to fill the rosters of NHL teams. There were just too many openings. Opportunity awaited those hailing from other countries, specifically, the United States. Another major influence was the growth of international competition.

Since the 1970s, the NHL has gone through cycles. First there was the bloody Broad Street Bully era, followed by the speed era as championed by Montreal, followed by the New York Islander era of steady, defensive-minded players. The defensive style that was to become the hallmark of the Minnesota Wild was the result of years of evolution in the NHL but came about as the result of the success coach Herb Brooks had with his "Miracle on Ice" 1980 Olympic championship. The Olympics showed that (1) Europeans knew how to stickhandle and defend; (2) Americans could skate with the best of them, including the Russians; and (3) Minnesotans made up the majority of the Olympic champions.

The state of Minnesota is home to the nation's top-ranked men's and women's hockey programs. The state also boasts Division I NCAA hockey programs at Minnesota, UMD, St. Cloud State, MSU-Mankato and Bemidji State, in addition to eleven hockey-playing Division III colleges. There are 156 boys' high school teams in the state playing hockey as members of the Minnesota State High School League and 122 girls' hockey teams. Currently there are 188 indoor ice arenas in the state from Worthington to Babbitt and from Austin to Crookston, including 9 in St. Paul.

Far from the days when Tommy Williams was the only Minnesotan playing in the NHL, there are, on average, forty Minnesota men today playing on NHL rinks throughout the league. More than any other state, Minnesota supplies the NHL with players. This is in addition to the sixty-some Minnesota natives in the American Hockey League. Others can be found in the ECHL, the Central Hockey League, the Southern Professional League and the Federal Hockey League. More can be located across Europe playing for hockey teams in various leagues such as the Kontinental Hockey League, Liiga (Finland), Deutsche Eishockey Liga, the Elite Ice Hockey League (UK) and the Swedish Hockey League.

A total of eight hockey players on the 2014 U.S. Olympic team hailed from Minnesota, more than from any other state.

History notes that, in addition to Americans, Swedes were the first interlopers in Canada's national game. While Ulf Sterner lasted only four games with the New York Rangers in 1954, Thommie Bergman joined the Detroit Red Wings in 1972 and stayed until 1980. In 1973, Borje Salming and Inge Hammarstrom signed with the Maple Leafs.

Since Canadians felt their jobs were in jeopardy when another wave of Swedish players arrived, the newcomers frequently encountered hostility in the NHL. But the Swedish infiltration was aided by the new job openings created by the World Hockey Association. Bobby Hull on the Winnipeg Jets was joined on a line with Swedes Anders Hedberg and Ulf Nilsson. The Oilers were to go on to import Finland's greatest skater, Jari Kurri. Later, the incomparable Teemu Selanne joined the Jets.

More Finns and Swedes arrived, displaying a free-flowing creative style of hockey that eschewed the dump-and-chase Canadian style. After the Swedes and the Finns came the Czechs, the Slovaks, the Russians, the Austrians and the Swiss.

Given that atmosphere, it was no wonder that the Minnesota Wild selected on June 24, 2000, as their first-ever amateur draft pick Marion Gaborik of Trencin, Slovakia. Also selected were Czech Lubomir Sekeras and Russian Maxim Sushinsky. The pair, along with Finns Antti Laaksonen and Kai Nurminen; Czechs Filip Kuba, Pavel Patera and Ladislav Benysek; Russian Sergei Krivokrasov; and South Korean Richard Park, would add a distinct international flare to the Wild's first year.

A trio of University of Minnesota graduates and state natives—Darby Hendrickson (Richfield), Jeff Nielsen (Grand Rapids) and Brian Bonin (St. Paul)—were on the Wild's first-year roster, as was American Jim Dowd of Brick, New Jersey.

The NHL expansion draft yielded goalie Jamie McLennan from the St. Louis Blues; left wing Scott Pellerin, also from St. Louis; center Stacy Roest

Dependable Finnish star Mikko Koivu (9) joined the Wild in 2005. The team captain, Koivu is on the ice for both power plays and penalty kills. *Walt Berry photo.*

from Detroit; defenseman Sean O'Donnell from the Los Angeles Kings; and forward Steve McKenna, also from Los Angeles. General manager Risebrough signed ace centerman Wes Walz as a free agent and traded with Dallas to get goaltender Manny Fernandez. It didn't hurt Fernandez's chances that he was the nephew of coach Lemaire.

On March 20, 2000, the Wild announced the sale of its 12,000th season ticket. Poor season-ticket sales were a contributing factor in the downfall of both the Minnesota North Stars and the Minnesota Fighting Saints. *St. Paul Pioneer Press* columnist Charley Walters noted that "eighty percent" of North Stars' season-ticket sales "came from Minneapolis and suburbs. With the St. Paul–based Wild, season tickets are split fifty-fifty between Minneapolis, St. Paul and their respective suburbs."

On June 15, 2000, the Wild and Xcel Energy announced a long-term naming rights partnership that saw the team's new arena christened the Xcel Energy Center. A "topping off" ceremony was held in the fall of 1999 as the 650,000-square-foot building was enclosed. With a roof in place, the construction team was able to work through the harsh winter months on the arena's interior features, which include seventy-four luxury suites. To commissioner Bettman's satisfaction, approximately three thousand club seats were located on the third level of the five-level edifice. Because of the relatively small footprint, 650,000 square feet, five seating levels were stacked inside. Four of the levels are for the public, and the fifth accommodates newspaper, television and radio personnel. Since seat levels are stacked, all spectators are provided with excellent views of game action.

Rink level is thirty-three feet below street level. The ice itself remains hard, thanks to nearly twelve miles of cooling pipes. The exterior of the Xcel Energy is glass, creating a feeling of openness and welcome. Building architect was the Kansas City firm HOK Sport, and at the time of its construction, the Xcel Energy Center was regarded as the finest hockey palace in the world. Seating capacity is listed at 18,064.

The team that Risebrough and Lemaire put on the ice for the 2000–01 season was one that did not shame its opulent surroundings. Lemaire believed in a defensive style of hockey, and he brought his neutral zone trap system with him from New Jersey. Consequently, the Wild, while lacking in goal-scorers, were seldom out of depth due to the resolute defense ethos Lemaire instilled.

Opening night was on October 11, 2000, against the Philadelphia Flyers, one of four Expansion Six franchises still operating in its city of origin. The game was a sellout, as would be the case with the next 409 games in team history, including 369 regular-season games, 27 pre-season matches and 13 playoff contests.

Fittingly, the first Wild goal was scored by Minnesotan Darby Hendrickson, now an assistant coach with the team. The game, played before a sellout crowd in the days before shootouts, ended in a 3–3 tie.

The team didn't win until October 18, an uncharacteristic 6–5 triumph over the Tampa Bay Lightning. Due to Lemaire's stressing smothering defense, most games in that first season were 2–1, 3–1 or 3–2 affairs.

The league had plopped the team in a division with three western Canada teams (Vancouver, Calgary and Edmonton) plus the Colorado Avalanche, based in Denver. From the viewpoint of the lords of the NHL, Minnesotans wore cowboy hats and boots. Travel proved taxing for Wild players since Minnesota was the only one of the five teams located in the Central Time Zone, and the fledgling team had little bench strength. At the time, few fans cared. The important fact was that Minnesota was back in the NHL.

Chapter 19

SEASONS OF CHANGE

The Minnesota Wild held fourth place for a few games that first November, but a 1–0 loss at home to Calgary dropped them to fifth, where they stayed until season's end. The Wild finished with 25 wins, 39 losses, 13 ties and 5 overtime losses. This contrasts with the 8-67-5 record of the Washington Capitals in their first year of existence and the 10-70-4 mark of the Ottawa Senators in that team's inaugural season. For the record, the Minnesota North Stars' first season produced 27 wins, 32 losses and 15 ties.

For a team short of goal-scorers, Gaborik, Hendrickson and Waltz each tallied eighteen. Pellerin was assist leader with twenty-eight. In goal, Fernandez was the most effective with a 19-14-4 mark and a 2.24 goals-against average. A milestone was reached on November 26, when Laaksonen scored the Wild's first-ever hat trick in a 4–2 win over Vancouver. A January 12 game versus Colorado drew a standing-room-only crowd of 18,815 spectators.

Win or lose, the metropolitan area fell in love with the new team. Tickets were hard to get, and Christmas sales of replica jerseys topped those of even the Vikings. More than a few North Stars replica jerseys were even purchased.

The 2001–02 season was a mirror image of the first, but this one sported an 11-9-5 record on December 2, good for third place. That quickly passed, and the team settled into fifth place for the balance of the season. But Marion Gaborik was emerging as a star in the league with thirty goals and thirty-seven assists for sixty-seven points, second only to newcomer Andrew Brunette, who had twenty-one goals and forty-eight assists for sixty-nine points.

In its third season, the Minnesota Wild reached a dizzying pinnacle, a feat that the team has yet to duplicate. By far the most fruitful of the Lemaire years was the 2002–03 season, remembered fondly as the "good old days" in Wild lore. The team raced to a 16-7-6 mark and held first place in the NHL's Northwest Division on December 12, 2002. From there until season's finish, Minnesota was never lower than third place in the standings, finishing with 42 wins, 29 losses, 10 ties and a single overtime loss. Xcel Energy Center records revealed forty-one consecutive sellouts, with an average crowd size of 18,501. Gaborik was all-everything for the Wild in goals, assists and points (sixty-five). Goalie Dwayne Roloson had 23 wins and a goals-against average of 2.0.

The euphoria of simply making the playoffs soon gave way to the goal of actually winning the playoffs. In defeating the Colorado Avalanche four games to three, the Wild became the eighth team in league history to win its first playoff series. To accomplish this, the club had to overcome a three-games-to-one deficit and win Games Five and Seven at the Pepsi Center in Denver.

Brunette was the hero, scoring the series-clinching goal, beating Patrick Roy at 3:25 of overtime in Game Seven. Hall of Famer Roy never played a game in goal after that and now is coach of the Avalanche. Roy remains the only player to win the Conn Smythe Trophy on three separate occasions (1986, 1993 and 2001). Brunette later played for the Avalanche and now is employed by the Wild as hockey operations advisor.

The next round of the playoffs moved to General Motors Place in Vancouver, where the Wild lost the opener 4–3. Minnesota rebounded to take the second game, 3–2, before the series shifted to St. Paul. There, the Wild luck seemed to run out. The Canucks won Game Three, and before the next game, Vancouver tough guy Todd Bertuzzi observed Wild fans standing in line waiting to purchase tickets for a possible Game Six. The roughneck Bertuzzi yelled to them not to bother because his team would make sure there wouldn't be a Game Six. The incident was reported to the media, thus ensuring that throughout the remainder of his career, no matter what uniform he wore, Bertuzzi would be roundly booed at the Xcel Energy Center. And thus, a Wild/Canucks rivalry was born.

As it turned out, Bertuzzi was wrong. There was a Game Six and a Game Seven, too. Amazingly, for the second straight Stanley Cup playoff series, the Wild overcame a three-games-to-one deficit by winning the fifth, sixth and seventh games. Only the sixth game was played on home ice, but no matter. Minnesota took care of business by the scores of 7–2, 5–1 and 4–2. Local hero Darby Hendrickson got the game-winning goal in the seventh and final game of the Vancouver series. Goalie Dwayne Roloson made twenty-four saves.

The Wild became the first team in NHL history to come back from a three-games-to-one deficit twice in the same Stanley Cup postseason and also became only the second club ever to win two seventh games on the road in the same playoff year. This was a fairy-tale season, but the magic didn't last.

In the playoffs, a hot goaltender can be the difference between winners and losers. And the Anaheim Mighty Ducks had a hot goaltender in J.S. Giguere, who shut out Minnesota 1–0 in the opener and 2–0 in the second game, both at the Xcel Energy Center. By Game Three, it was apparent that merely scoring on Giguere would be a victory of sorts, but that would have to wait for the next game, as the Wild fell, this time by the score of 4–0.

Brunette was able to get that elusive Wild goal in the Game Four, and it gave Minnesota a 1–0 lead, but that was all. Two Adam Oates goals put Minnesota away, and Anaheim advanced while the Wild players packed their bags and headed to their summer homes. Giguere had turned back 122 out of 123 shots fired on him for the series.

Those who thought the Wild had nowhere to go but up in 2003–04 were wrong. The team fell to last place on February 22 and stayed there. Then something unprecedented happened. There was no 2004–2005 season. Bettman and the owners locked out players from competition for an entire season until a new collective bargaining agreement could be worked out. Many players, particularly Europeans, left for the season to play abroad.

For whatever reason, the Minnesota Wild was not the same team after a year's lockout. A particularly dire omen was the death during the lockout due to heart failure of Sergei Zholtok on the ice in a game in Europe. Zholtok died in the arms of teammate Darby Hendrickson.

The Wild, along with the other NHL teams, returned to the ice for the 2005–06 season, but the magic of the 2003 playoff team was missing. Last place became the Wild home after the eighteenth regular-season game. Brian Rolston did set a team record with seventy-nine points, and Gaborik had a personal-best thirty-eight goals.

Like a bad dream, when Minnesota did finally make it back into the Stanley Cup playoffs, who was waiting for them but the dreaded Ducks of Anaheim, no longer mighty but mighty enough to subdue the Wild in five games. The Wild scored only nine goals in the series, three of which were tallied by Gaborik. The season did witness the coming of age of a pair

Goalie Niklas Backstrom came out of nowhere to team with Manny Fernandez and win the 2007 William Jennings Trophy in 2007. *Walt Berry photo.*

of Finnish stars: centerman Mikko Koivu and goalie Niklas Backstrom. Koivu tallied fifty-four points while appearing in all eighty-two Wild games. Backstrom teamed with Fernandez to win the 2007 William Jennings Trophy as the Wild allowed a league-low 191 goals.

On December 7, 2007, Craig Leipold completed the sale of the Nashville Predators for $193 million. He had been the team's owner since Nashville was granted a NHL franchise in 1997, paying $80 million for the privilege. Leipold was a "Wisconsin businessman who had married into the SC Johnson household products empire," according to Jonathan Gatehouse in this biography of commissioner Gary Bettman. "By 2002–03, Nashville had the worst attendance in the league" with "cumulative losses approaching $70 million and revenues of just $45 million."

Leipold, from Racine, Wisconsin, had attempted to sell the Predators to Canadian Jim Balsillie for $220 million, but when that fell through, he accepted $193 million from a group of local Nashville boys. Leipold then purchased the Minnesota Wild for $250 million. A new broom frequently sweeps clean, and eventually Risebrough, Lemaire and Robertson were gone.

On May 22, 2009, Chuck Fletcher was named general manager of the Minnesota Wild, replacing Risebrough. Fletcher was named to oversee the club's hockey operations department, including all matters relating to the Wild's player personnel, coaching staff, scouting department and minor-league operations. A Harvard graduate, Fletcher is the son of Cliff Fletcher, longtime NHL general manager. Chuck Fletcher was hired by Leipold from the Pittsburgh Penguins, where he was serving as assistant general manager.

The current Minnesota Wild coach is Mike Yeo, who has held that position since June 17, 2011. Yeo, who never played in the NHL, previously was coach of Minnesota's Houston farm club. *Walt Berry photo*.

Lemaire's retirement at the end of the 2008–09 season brought about the team's first coaching change. To replace the popular Jacques, Fletcher brought in University of Minnesota alumnus Todd Richards. The team had lost its singular star, Marion Gaborik, to free agency and struggled throughout the 2009–10 season, finishing fourth in the Northwest and thirteenth overall in the West Conference. Koivu was now team leader with seventy-one points.

Another season passed with little improvement, and Richards was gone, replaced by Mike Yeo, previously coach of the farm team Houston Aeros. Yeo had been an assistant coach of the Pittsburgh Penguins prior to moving to Houston. Yeo, like his predecessor, was unable to reach the playoffs.

By 2012, Leipold realized that something was needed to boost attendance. The 2011–12 season had produced only sixteen sellout crowds out of forty-one home games.

The Wild made front-page news on July 4 when Leipold announced the signing of not one but two twenty-seven-year-old NHL superstars in a package deal. For $98 million each, Minnesota obtained the services of left-winger Zach Parise and defenseman Ryan Suter, both American-born players in high demand by at least a dozen other NHL teams.

Charley Walters, writing in the *St. Paul Pioneer Press*, observed that "between Parise and Suter, the Wild will have $196 million committed for 13 years in guaranteed contracts." Walters then interviewed Parise's father, J.P. Parise, regarding the nearly $100 million deal his son got. The elder Parise told Walters that in his nine seasons with the North Stars, the most he ever earned was "$100,000 a year."

The signing of Parise and Suter energized a previously lethargic fan base. Within a day of the announcement, five hundred new season tickets were sold. Two days later, the number had jumped beyond one thousand.

"This is a rare opportunity," said Fletcher, "for us to transform our franchise by adding two marquee players who are both in their prime, at the same time."

Parise grew up in Faribault, Minnesota, where his dad coached hockey at the exclusive Shattuck–St. Mary's High School. Suter, from Madison, Wisconsin, is married to a Bloomington, Minnesota woman. He played for the hometown University of Wisconsin's hockey team before being signed by the Nashville Predators.

Parise was reportedly advised to consider attending, among many schools, North Dakota University in Grand Forks by none other than Herb Brooks, a move that, when announced by a Grand Forks newspaper writer, shocked followers of the University of Minnesota hockey program. What we do know about the veracity of the Brooks story is that Parise did indeed enroll at North Dakota and played there for two hockey seasons before signing with the New Jersey Devils.

The money Parise and Suter will earn makes the $2 million cost of a North Stars expansion franchise look like small change. A look at the contracts of both players reveals payments to each of $12 million for the first two seasons, $11 million for the next, $9 million for the next five, $8 million for 2020–21, $6 million for 2021–22, $2 million for the following season and $1 million for the last two.

"The Wild suddenly became relevant," wrote Bob Sansevere in the *St. Paul Pioneer Press*, "going from a team that was hoping to make the playoffs to a team expected to go deep into the postseason."

But all that would have to wait. Once again, labor strife reared its ugly head in the NHL. As had happened in the 2004–05 season, opening games were called off because the owners locked out their players. At stake was the issue of revenue sharing. The National Hockey League Players Association (NHLPA) knew that Bettman was capable of shutting down hockey for another full season, if necessary, and this was a potent bargaining chip. Bettman and the owners wanted a fifty-fifty revenue sharing split, and they

Wild owner Craig Leipold shocked the hockey world when he signed Americans Zach Parise (left) and Ryan Suter to identical $98 million contracts. Parise is the son of former North Star J.P. Parise. *Walt Berry photo.*

got it at the cost of thirty-four cancelled regular-season games per team.

Thus, the season didn't get underway until January 19, 2013. The Wild's forty-eight-game schedule was confined to competition against only teams from the West. The scheduling wrinkle meant that, once again, a lockout had discombobulated the team's progress. In 2004, it had derailed any momentum gained from playoff success. Now, because there were no pre-season games, it killed the Wild's opportunity to gradually adjust to life with a pair of superstars.

Minnesota went through fits and spurts in the truncated season, waiting until the final day to cinch the eighth and final spot in the West. For the first game of the Stanley Cup playoffs, the Wild drew the number-one seed, the Chicago Blackhawks, once the nemesis of the North Stars. Minnesota's chances were greatly diminished when goalie Backstrom was injured during pre-game warm-ups at the United Center. Without Backstrom, the Wild lost the opener 2–1 on April 30, and on May 3, with Josh Harding in goal, fell once again to the mighty Blackhawks by the score of 5–2. Minnesota did recover at home on the Xcel Energy Center ice to win 3–2, with Jason Zucker getting the game-winning goal. But Chicago brushed that aside and won Games Four and Five by scores of 3–0 and 5–1 to take the series.

The next season would see the realignment of the NHL into four divisions (from six) with, improbably, sixteen teams in the East and fourteen in the West. This happened in the same year that Major League Baseball finally came to its senses and switched to a balanced fifteen-and-fifteen setup. But then there's never a rational accounting for NHL intelligence. The Wild did benefit, however, by being slotted in the West with Winnipeg, Chicago, St. Louis, Colorado, Nashville and the former North Stars, now the Dallas plain

Star of the future for the Wild is hustling lefty centerman Mikael Granlund, already a household name in his native Finland, where freelance photographers follow his every move. *Walt Berry photo*.

old Stars. The West did, however, lose Detroit, which means that five of the Original Six are now in the East. Of the remaining five teams of the Expansion Six, three franchises (Los Angeles, St. Louis and Dallas) are in the West.

No longer grouped with Vancouver, Edmonton and Calgary, the Wild nevertheless struggled with player injury and illness in the 2013–14 season and desperately attempted to hold on to the eighth-place playoff berth.

At the end of the regular season, Minnesota's ninety-eight points ranked eleventh among the sixteen teams in the NHL Stanley Cup hunt. The Wild posted a record of 14-4-2 from January 2 through March 3 and earned a fourth-place playoff spot in the Central Division playoffs, where Minnesota defeated the Colorado Avalanche in seven games before losing in the second round to Chicago by four games to two.

INDEX

About the Author

A sports historian and author, George Rekela is the retired executive editor of *Construction Bulletin Magazine*, *Concrete Pumping* and *Burlington Northern News*. A journalism graduate of the University of Minnesota, he has authored more than a dozen sports and construction industry books. He is a past president of the Halsey Hall Chapter of the Society for American Baseball Research (SABR) and a member of the Society for International Hockey Research (SIHR).

Visit us at
www.historypress.net

··

This title is also available as an e-book

CPSIA information can be obtained
at www.ICGtesting.com
Printed in the USA
LVHW081515201222
735620LV00004B/342

9 781540 209665